Sea Creatures

Photo Fact Collection

Table of Contents

Photo Credits: Fish

Dr. E.R. Degginger: pages 9, 10, 19, 22, 26
Al Grotell: pages 8, 11, 13, 16, 18, 20, 24, 26
Kit Kittle: pages 23, 24
Aaron Norman: pages 25, 26, 27
Herb Segars: page 9
American Fisheries Society: pages 8, 10, 12, 13, 16, 22, 23, 29
Rod & Kathy Canham/WaterHouse: pages 15, 19, 21
Barbara Doernbach/WaterHouse: page 28
Stephen Frink/WaterHouse: pages 9, 11, 12, 14, 18, 21, 24, 25, 28
Robert Holland/WaterHouse: page 13
Carl Roessler/WaterHouse: pages 18, 20
Marty Snyderman/WaterHouse: pages 16, 29

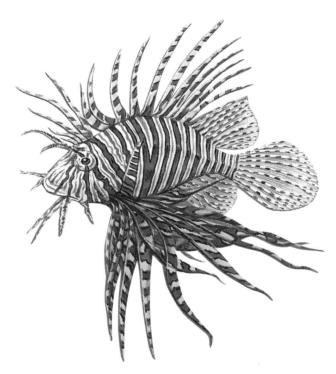

Front Cover: Creatas
End Pages: front - Steven Frink/Waterhouse; back - Robin Lee Makowski

FISH

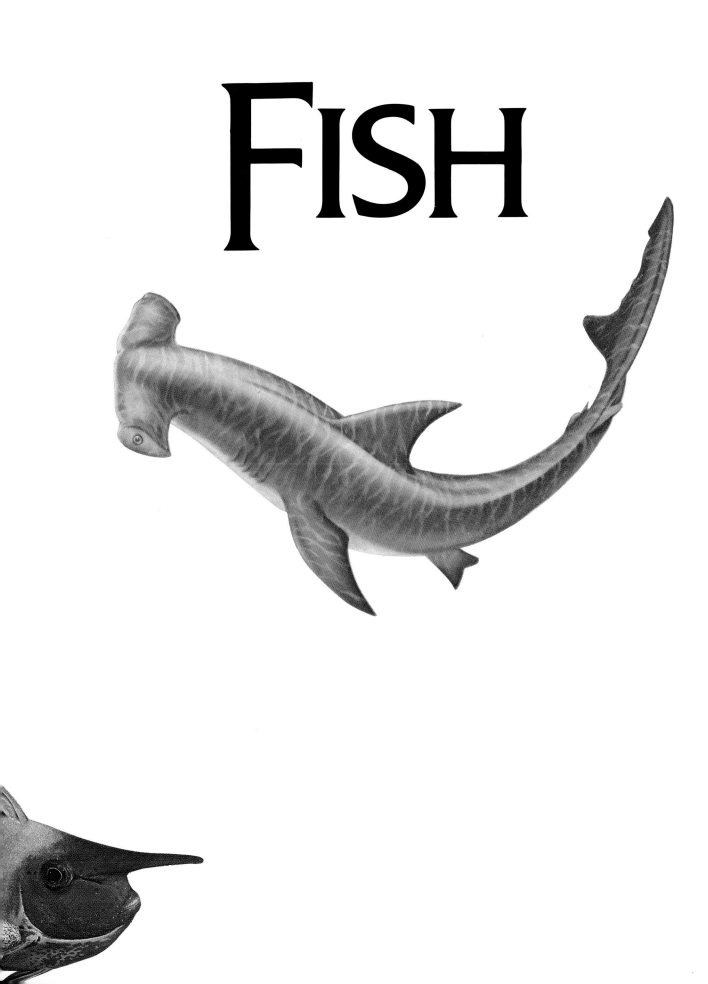

FISH STORY

Water covers approximately 75% of the earth's surface. In it swim billions of fish from over 25,000 species. Fish are cold-blooded. Their blood temperature changes with the temperature of the surrounding water. Fish can live in a warm lake in summer and stay in that same ice-covered lake in winter.

Water Works

A fish is naturally equipped to live in water. It has gills for taking oxygen from the water, and a swim bladder, like a balloon, to keep it afloat. By changing the amount of air in its bladder, a fish never rises or sinks, but stays balanced.

Dorsal Fin ———

Pectoral Fin

Gill Cover

Breathing

A fish "breathes in" by passing water through its mouth. The gill covers close to keep the water in. Then the gills remove the oxygen and pass it into the bloodstream. To "breathe out," the mouth closes tightly and the gill covers open to let water out.

Armed With Scales

A fish's overlapping scales are called "armor" because they protect the fish. Mucous, a slimy substance, moistens the scales, protects them from infection, and helps the fish slip through the water faster.

Pelvic Fin

◀ Sensitive Nose

Fish have openings on their snouts that do the work of human nostrils. The paddlefish has a super-long snout armed with nerves and sense organs that detect food. When it's hungry, all the paddlefish has to do is follow its nose.

Functional Fins

Fins move the fish forward, steer it, and maintain balance. The pectoral and pelvic fins are used for balance, steering, and braking. The dorsal fin keeps the fish from rolling over and works along with the anal fin to act as a stabilizer. The tail fin provides power, thrusting the fish forward.

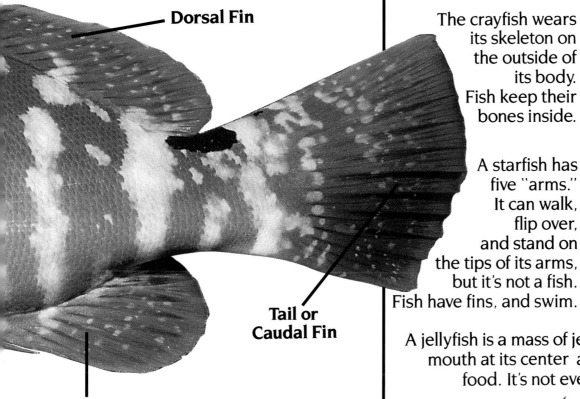

Dorsal Fin

Tail or Caudal Fin

Anal Fin

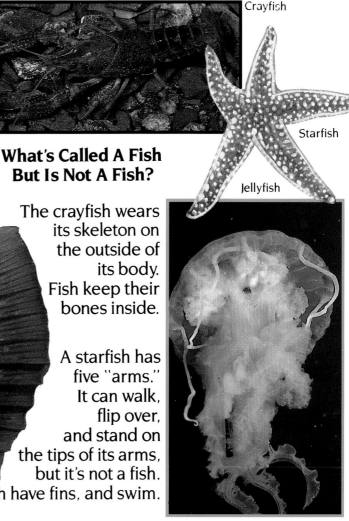

Crayfish

Starfish

Jellyfish

What's Called A Fish But Is Not A Fish?

The crayfish wears its skeleton on the outside of its body. Fish keep their bones inside.

A starfish has five "arms." It can walk, flip over, and stand on the tips of its arms, but it's not a fish. Fish have fins, and swim.

A jellyfish is a mass of jelly-like material with a mouth at its center and tentacles to gather food. It's not even close to being a fish!

Along the sides of a fish are the sense organs that help it swim around invisible objects in muddy water or keep perfect formations in a school.

Swimming In Style

To swim forward, fish sweep their bodies from side to side. The curve they make is a snake-like motion that goes from head to tail, with the tail giving the most kick. Some fish are faster than others, and the sailfish, who swims at about 60 miles an hour, is the speed demon of the sea.

WATER WAYS

Fish are the way they are because they live in the water. Water has given them their shape, their way of breathing, and their method of moving and feeding. But water has a variety of temperatures and currents, saltiness and freshness, shallows and depths, animal and plant life. Fish have adapted to these different environments. Some fish even live in pools that dry up for long periods of time. So as different as the water is, fish are different, too.

Fish Families
There are three basic types of fish.

Sea Lamprey

Jawless fish are hagfish and sea lampreys. They are primitive, snake-like, and scaleless. Their round mouths are like suction cups lined with more than 100 sharp teeth. This gruesome twosome stays alive by sucking the blood and body fluids out of other fish.

Sea Lamprey Mouth

Shark

Sharks, rays, and skates have skeletons made of **cartilage**, not bone. Your ears and the soft "bone" in your nose are made of cartilage.

The **bony** fish are all the rest, from a little guppy to a giant tuna. All these fish have a skeleton made of bone, the same as mammals, reptiles, and birds.

Guppy

10

◀ **Long Distance Swimmer**
Fresh or saltwater? There are a few unusual fish that can live in both. The salmon begins its spectacular journey in the freshwater river where it was born. At three years old and about ten inches long, the fish starts downstream to the salty sea. After four or five years, and weighing up to 20 pounds, the salmon returns to spawn (lay its eggs) at the place where it was born. It struggles fiercely against the current, waterfalls, dams, and predators, arriving at its birthplace bruised and exhausted, but ready to reproduce.

Rock Bass

Yellow Perch

Sunfish

Trout

How Fresh!
Perch, trout, bass, and sunfish are the most common fish found in freshwater rivers and lakes.

Viperfish

The saltwater seas are vast. But most fish live close to the shore where the water is less than 600 feet deep. In the ocean, the deeper the water, the dimmer the light. Many fish who live at 2,000 feet or deeper face the dark with light-producing cells called photophores. Blinking along in the blackness, the viperfish is equipped with the lights and teeth it needs to repel enemies or attract prey.

Whale Shark

▲ Meal Plan

The food chain refers to what animals eat. Big fish eat smaller ones and smaller ones eat tiny ones. The tiny ones eat plankton — microscopic plants and animals that drift in the currents in incredible numbers. Plankton, at the bottom of the food chain, is also eaten by the largest fish in the sea, the whale shark. This 50 foot, 40,000 pound giant doesn't eat other fish — only tons and tons of plankton.

Tropical Beauty ▶

Beauty may be only skin deep, but tropical fish have it. These fish live in warm waters among coral reefs, darting in and out of the coral to escape predators. They're small, swift, and decorated with stripes, spots, and colors that seem too beautiful to be true.

NAME THAT FISH

Fish have scientific names which place them in families so they can be studied in groups with similar characteristics. They also have common names. Here are some fish that have good reasons for their common names. They're funny, odd, peculiar, weird, and their names say it all.

▲ Filefish

Some fish are named for their shape, but the filefish is named for its skin. The skin of this fish is so hard and rough, it has been used as sandpaper — a useful fish!

▲ Flathead

The hammerhead shark has a head like a flattened bar — a hammer's head — with an eye and a nostril on each end. Other fish must wonder where the hammerhead is looking.

Can you guess why I'm called a unicorn fish?

▲ Triggerfish

The triggerfish has a fin-shaped "trigger," and it actually works. The trigger is created by locking the spines of its dorsal fin. A frightened triggerfish dives into coral and uses its spine to anchor itself where enemies can't reach it. So to be safe, this fish has got to be quick on the trigger.

◀ Nasty Needles

Sawfish
is the perfect name for this member of the ray family.

Needle fish are silvery and skinny, and about six feet long. Slicing through the surface of the water, they look like, of course, needles. The needle fish uses its sharp teeth to snatch small fish and juggle them into a head-first position in its mouth. Then (slurp!) it swallows them whole.

With a nose that could clear a forest, what *else* could it be called? Its saw-like snout, about one-third the fish's length, has 24 to 32 teeth. In a 20 foot sawfish, the saw can be six feet long!

Cowfish ▼
The smallest creature to be called a cow has got to be the cowfish. Only one foot long, this fish got its name from the two cow-like horns that stick out of its head.

▲ Toothless Terror
The upper jaw of the swordfish grows and grows until it's a dangerous sword. A real slasher, the swordfish storms into a school of fish and rips its sword through whatever it can. Then, the eating begins … but not the chewing. The mighty swordfish, who can drive its sword through a wooden boat, has no teeth.

13

FISH DISGUISES

Fish don't play hide and seek. They hide to live and seek to eat. Nearly all fish hide from their enemies and some use disguises to prey on others. Color and shape are the most important parts of a fish's disguise. With all the fish in the sea, imagine how many colors and shapes there must be!

Seaweed Safety▲

The sargassum fish is named for the seaweed it swims in. This is no wonder because the colors match perfectly. These tiny fish anchor themselves to the seaweed with "fingers" at the end of their fins. There they safely sit where no one can see them.

▲ Clear Sailing

The see-through body of this fish is so transparent, that it's very difficult to see its shape. If it can't be seen, it can't be caught.

Ganging Up

Fish with bright stripes are not dressed up, they're disguised. When a big fish sees this school of grunts for example, all it sees are stripes, not heads or tails. If the grunts dart quickly in all directions, their enemy becomes even more confused—and finally, goes away hungry.

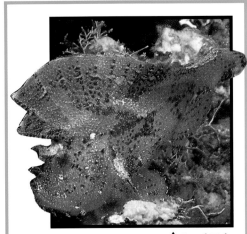

Lethal Disguises　▲ Leaf Fish

A leaf fish lurking among the leaves is practically unseen, while the frog fish is disguised to look like a piece of red coral. A smaller fish wouldn't even know these deadly predators were in town until (gulp!) it was too late.

▼ Frog Fish

▼ Spellbinder

This weird outfit belongs to the lionfish. Its enemies don't see a clear outline of the lion and don't know exactly what they are looking at. Little fish seem to be hypnotized by the spooky sight of the lionfish. They stay still and tremble, making them easy prey for a hungry lion.

▲ The Eyes Have It

Some fish have false "eyespots" near their tails to fool predators. The eyespot is larger than the real eye, so the enemy thinks the fish is too big to eat, and that gives the butterfly fish a better chance of getting away—quick as a wink.

◀ Stoneface

A scorpion fish has a large, turned down mouth and warty growths all over its body. But being ugly is beautiful for the scorpion because it looks exactly like a rock with seaweed growing over it. All the scorpion fish has to do for dinner is open its mouth and wait for a fish to swim in.

Master of Disguise

If you think you're looking at the ocean floor in these pictures, you better look again. What you're really seeing is a flounder, a flatfish that can change the color and pattern of its markings to look like the ground it lays on. These talented flounders can hide from their predators or remain unnoticed by their own prey.

SEA HORSES

The odd and beautiful sea horse has a head like a delicate horse, a grasping tail like a monkey, an outer skeleton like an insect, and a pouch like a kangaroo. With all these borrowed parts, the sea horse doesn't look like a real fish, or act much like a fish, either. Still, the tiny sea horse **is** a true fish.

Swimming Motion

A sea horse swims like the leader of a very dignified parade. Vibrating its barely noticeable fins like mad — as fast as 35 times a second — the sea horse seems to grandly glide by.

All Bones

The sea horse has bones inside *and* out. It has an inner skeleton like all bony fish — and an outer skeleton of bony plates. When a sea horse dies and dries out, its skeleton keeps its shape. People are so fascinated by the appearance of this odd fish, that dried sea horses are used in ornaments and jewelry.

Eyes Apart

The sea horse's eyes work independently of each other. One eye can look forward to see what's coming, while the other looks backward to see what's behind. It's hard to hide from a sea horse.

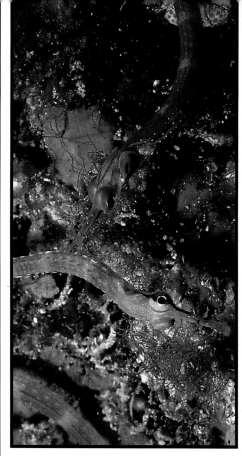

Stringbean ▲

A pipefish is not a sea horse that's been stretched or starved. It's just a skinny relative of the sea horse.

◄ Vacuum System

Whoosh! Click! The sea horse eats with its long tube-like snout which has a tiny trap door at the end. Whoosh! The snout vacuums up tiny forms of sea life. Click! The trap door closes. The sea horse may not have any teeth, but it does have a horse's appetite.

▼ Baby sea horses are born as fully developed miniatures of their parents. The female deposits her eggs in the male's kangaroo-like pouch and goes on her way. He carries the eggs for about six weeks until the babies— as many as 200—emerge.

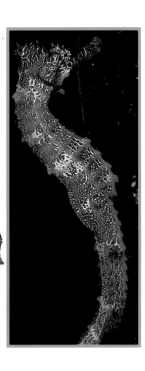

Helpful Tail
Most fish swim with the aid of their tails, but not the sea horse. Its tail is long and thin and has no fin— it's more like a hand than a tail. The sea horse coils its tail into a tight spiral, grabbing onto seaweed and coral where it can stay still for hours. Sometimes two sea horses lock tails and have a tug-of-war.

▲ **Seaweed Sea Horse**
Sea horses can change color to match their surroundings. But the award for best camouflage goes to the leafy sea dragon from Australia. It has amazing skin flaps that make it look much more like seaweed than a sea horse.

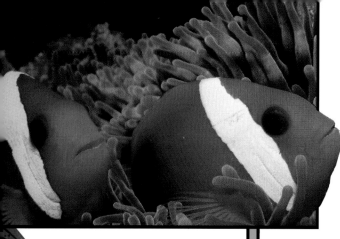

DEFENSE

Most fish are both hunted and hunter. That is, while they are searching for smaller fish to eat, someone is hoping to have **them** for dinner. How can a fish defend itself? Some have physical characteristics that put off their enemies. For example, no one is going to attack a fish with poisonous spines if they can help it. But, they may not know that until it's too late.

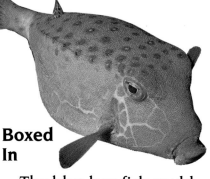

Boxed In

The blue box fish could be a turtle's cousin. It's covered with a tortoise-like shell except where its fins, eyes, and tail stick out. No bigger fish wants to take a bite out of this hard-head.

▲ The little clownfish lives among the stinging tentacles of the sea anemone, which looks like a plant, but is really an animal. The clownfish is immune to the anemone's sting, so swimming among the wavy arms of its friend, the clownfish is completely safe.

Sea Surgeon

Surgeon fish carry razor-sharp barbs at the base of their tails. These blades can be aimed —raised and pointed forward—so that a fish passing by can be slashed, sliced, or slit. As for people, the surgeon fish will gladly operate on anyone who grabs it by the tail.

Tough ▶ Puff

If attacked, a porcupine fish has a great defense. It's equipped with needle sharp spines all over its body, *and* it can swallow water or air to puff itself up into a prickly balloon. A big porcupine looks like a basketball spiked with nails. Now **that** would be tough to swallow.

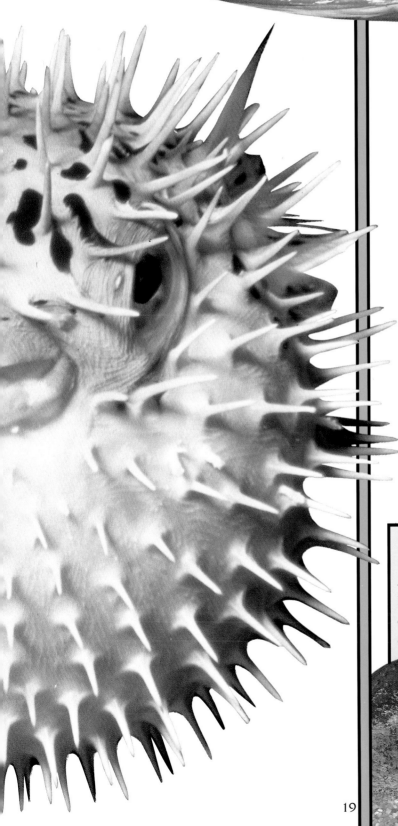

▲ Barracuda

The barracuda is a fish whose best defense is an attack—on man or fish. A smiling barracuda is all sharp teeth and frightening fangs. If these teeth are worn or broken, new ones grow in to take their place. Not all barracuda are dangerous, but it never makes sense to trust one. Even if it's smiling.

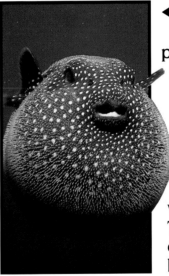

◄ Fish Ball

A puffer, like the porcupine fish, escapes from its enemies by puffing itself up.

An inflated puffer will bob on the surface like a balloon.

Few fish can get their mouths around a puffer when it's so roly-poly. That's the best part of being a beautiful, bouncing ball of fish.

Shocking Defense

What's a cross between a cat and a light bulb? An electric catfish, of course. This fish defends itself with wicked electric shocks that come from a coat of tissue beneath its skin. That means that all four feet of the electric catfish are a shocking experience to any creature that comes near it.

19

RAYS

Cousins to the shark, rays look as if they had been run over by a sea-going steamroller. Their pectoral fins are enlarged and attached to their heads, forming wing-like shapes. When they wave their fins up and down, they move through water like huge, elegant birds. Like sharks, a ray's skeletal system is made of cartilage. Unlike sharks, rays are not aggressive — but they can be dangerous.

▼The eyes of a
ray are on *top*
of its head.
But the mouth and gills are on the *bottom*.
To breathe, water comes in through two
openings behind the eyes and goes out
through the gills. The ray's eyesight
is good and its nose, at the tip,
is excellent. Its mouth is perfect for
scooping up shellfish, crabs, and small
fish on the ocean floor. So with this
totally flattened, two-faced
technique, the ray goes
on its way quite well.

▲ Spotted Skate
Skates are members of the ray family. When they swim, they move their pectoral fins from front to back instead of "flapping" them like rays.

Manta Ray ▶

The giant manta ray measures as much as 20 feet across and can weigh up to 3,000 pounds. Unlike bottom dwellers, mantas cruise the water's surface eating plankton, small plant and animal organisms. Sometimes, by flapping its spectacular "wings," a manta ray can "fly" 15 feet out of the water.

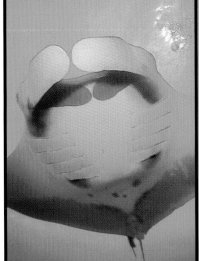

Spine Story ▼

A stringray, like most rays and skates, lays in shallow water covered with sand and minds its own business … unless someone *steps* on it. Then … Whap! … it swings its long tail and strikes with its spine. The single spine on the tail of a stingray is poisonous and dangerous. The wound can be just painful or paralyzing, depending on the size of the ray. Some rays even have spines that are replaced if they are lost.

◀ Blue-Spotted Ray

A Stingray's
▲ Poisonous Spine

Not A Shark

The guitarfish shows how closely related sharks and rays really are. It has a longer, thinner, more shark-like body, but its gills are on the underside of its body, so it's definitely a ray. The guitarfish's teeth are blunt, not sharp, but there are a lot of them — 65 or 70 rows.

Charged Up

The torpedo ray is one of the only fish with enough electric power to stun a man. Its electric charge is so well developed that its babies, which are born live, are able to produce electricity upon birth.

Guitarfish

TRICKY FISH

Tricky fish! They walk. They talk. They breathe and fly. They even hibernate. Who are they and how did they get this way? Slowly. Six hundred million years is the age of the oldest fossil fish found so far. Over the centuries, as fish changed and adapted to their surroundings, some of them developed bizarre, fantastic behaviors.

▲ Walking Underwater

Watch a sea robin move along the ocean floor and it seems to be walking. Six rays, three from each pectoral fin, stick out and poke around in the sand. This trickster can even "talk." By vibrating its swim bladder, it can produce a croaking sound.

▶ Fake Flyer

Flying fish don't really fly, but they do get airborne. Swimming very fast, they thrust their upper bodies out of the water, spread their fins and glide above the water. They can fly fifty yards in three seconds at 35 miles per hour!

Take Cover ▶

Here comes the archer fish squirting bullets. Insects are its prey and water is its weapon. Spotting a bug on a leaf, the archer gets in position, takes aim, and "shoots" drops of water at its victim. A sure shot at four feet, larger archer fish can propel water up to 12 feet.

Walking On Land

The frog-faced mudskipper can breathe on land. It carries water in its gills and returns to the water now and then to fill up. On the ground, the mudskipper struts along with its pectoral fins and even leaps by pushing off with its tail.

▲ Drum Roll!

Underwater music gets its beat from the drumfish who vibrates its bladder to make the noise it's named for—a drumming sound —and it can be loud. A school of drums playing around a ship can keep a crew up all night!

Remora ▶

A free ride is the remora's idea of a good day. This fish uses the powerful suction disk on top of its head to stick to other fish—preferably a shark. The suction of this two foot "shark sucker" is so strong that it has been known to lift 24 pounds. Now **that's** using its head!

Body Work ▼

Fish get infections and parasites and fungi. So who do they call? The cleaners. Cleaner fish do the dirty work of nibbling away their hosts' pests, parasites, bacteria, and dead skin. Some work around the sharp teeth, and even down the throats of some very scary fellows. This moray eel stays neat and tidy with the help of its cleaner friends.

Flying Hatchet ▲

Meet the only true flyer among fish, the tiny three inch hatchet fish, shaped like a food chopper. Whizzing along for about six feet, flapping its pectoral fins like mad, this fish actually **flies!** Huge chest muscles, a quarter of its weight, give the hatchet the power to take off.

EELS

In ancient times people thought that eels were related to snakes and worms. Eels, however, are true fish with fins and gills and scales. Many swim in both salt and fresh water, something most fish can't do. The most common eels are anywhere from one and a half to six feet long and live in lakes, river bottoms, harbors, and marshes.

Spotted Moray Eel

Eel Garden
What looks like a question mark, lives in colonies, and acts like a real stick-in-the-mud? The garden eel. Garden eels spend all their time stuck tail-first in holes on the ocean floor. They rarely leave their burrows and if danger comes, they sink right in up to their eyeballs. As many as a thousand may live together.

Slippery As An Eel
Eels have more mucous than most fish.

Spotted Spoon-Nose Eel

That might make an eel feel good, but it makes touching one a pretty slimy experience. This spotted spoon-nose eel is one of about 600 species of eels.

Irritable Eel ▲
The "rattlesnake of the sea" is the moray eel, a fish that is as vicious as it looks. There are many types of morays hiding in the nooks and crannies of coral reefs. Some are large, reaching up to ten feet and weighing 200 pounds. And some are poisonous — as if strong jaws, sharp teeth, and a powerful bite weren't enough.

A moray eel will hide in anything it can fit into, even this tube sponge.

24

▲ The Shocking Truth

The electric eel is a six foot long fish that swims in the rivers of South America. Most of its body is filled with special battery-like organs. A short blast of its electricity can stun a man and paralyze or kill small prey.

▲ Trip Of A Lifetime

Anguilla eels, the most common freshwater eels, live in inland lakes and rivers. These eels migrate, sometimes thousands of miles, to lay their eggs in the Sargasso Sea, an area in the Atlantic Ocean thick with seaweed. The babies that are born return to the same place their parents came from. These baby eels will become adults living in freshwater who will again return to the Sargasso Sea to spawn. No one knows why.

This spotted moray lets a cleaner shrimp pick its teeth. ▼

Early Stages

1.

2.

3.

In its infancy, an eel is a tiny, leaf-shaped creature. In childhood it becomes a "glass eel," a little see-through eel. Then it changes into an "elver," a small, black eel, probably a teenager in eel life.

AND BABY MAKES 3,000

To reproduce, fish "spawn," — the female places her eggs in the water, the male releases sperm and the eggs are fertilized. Most fish simply lay eggs and go on their way. But not all. Some build nests, dig pits, and find hiding places for their eggs. Eggs are good food for predators, but they are also the future for each fish species, so their survival is an important part of the fish story.

Not Clowning Around

This brightly colored clownfish guards its eggs near the safety provided by the sea anemone.

Surf and Birth ▲

The grunion rides the waves onto the beach. The female digs herself, tail first, into the soft, wet sand and lays her eggs. When she struggles free, the male fertilizes them. Then both wiggle toward the sea and catch a wave into deeper water. Two weeks later a high tide washes the eggs out. Two or three minutes in the water and the baby grunions are hatched and swimming on their own.

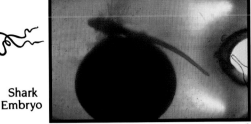

Cat Shark

Port Jackson Shark

Shark Embryo

An egg without any protection has a good chance of being eaten. Some sharks and skates lay their eggs in leathery cases. Each one is the home of just one egg. The case has hooks that catch onto seaweed or anchor on the bottom of the ocean. There it sits for several months while the egg develops safely into a fish.

▲ Countless Cod

Fish that lay few eggs usually guard them, or none might survive. The cod can lay four million or more eggs a year, and the parents just let them float away without so much as a tail-wave goodbye. But only one baby in every million needs to live to continue the survival of this fish. If they all survived, the seas would be clogged with cod.

Egg Laying
◀ Champion

The ocean sunfish can measure 12 feet from top to bottom and weigh 3,000 pounds. It lays more eggs than any other fish— as many as 300 million eggs at a time!

Safekeeping

Some fish search for a safe place for their eggs. The bitterling uses a place as safe as a bank vault—a mussel. To "deposit" her eggs in the mussel, the three-inch bitterling develops a tube. She uses the tube to place one or two eggs in a mussel and the male fertilizes them. Then the parent team moves on to another mussel, and another, making many safe deposits.

Toadfish Treasure ▼

Broken bottles, tin cans, boards, and plastic bottles—all these shouldn't be found on the ocean floor. But they are and the toadfish is glad. This fish thinks litter is an ideal nesting site. The male toadfish guards the nest ferociously. His treasure is hidden in the trash.

Baby fish are called "fry." Although many fish have no interest in their newly hatched offspring, some do. They may just hover around to fight off attackers, or keep the fry in specially built nests, or even carry them around in their mouths.

Under The Bull's Eye
Baby bullhead catfish have protective parents. The babies form a school and stay together. Like this mama bullhead catfish, the parents stay nearby and keep an eye on them until they're about two inches long— big enough to brave the world.

Mouth House
Tilapia babies hatch in their mother's mouth. The tiny fish may swim out now and then, but come right back when there's trouble. During this time, the "mouthbrooder," as this fish is called, gets pretty hungry. After a while, the fry may be safer on their own. If they swim back in, there's a good chance they could be swallowed!

Herring Hordes ▲
Silversides, as herring fry are called, hatch from sticky eggs that cling to stones, sand, and seaweed. Adult females, traveling in gigantic schools, lay their eggs at the same time, maybe 30,000 each. That's why there are so many herring in the world—they are one of the most numerous of all creatures with backbones.

The fry of this African jewelfish are ready to start life on their own.

F R Y

Bubble Nest ▶

The male siamese fighting fish builds a nest of bubbles on the water's surface. He carries each egg in his mouth and places it in the nest which constantly needs new bubbles. When the babies fall out and escape faster than he can return them, and there's no time to repair the nest, father knows his job is done.

▼ Angelfish

Newly hatched angelfish are stuck to their spawning place by a fine, sticky thread attached to their heads. If a baby does break free, a parent swoops down to put it back with the others. However, after about three or four days, the babies bust loose in bunches too large to lasso. Soon, the full grown angelfish are ready to raise fry of their own.

Babysitter

This fierce, male stickleback, two to four inches long, builds a nest for his fry and keeps them there. He tries to keep the babies from wandering off and may bring them back in his mouth. After about two weeks, the nest is worn out and so is dad.

▶ And The Winner Is...

Who gets the Mother and Father of the Sea Award? The discus fish, of course. These super parents don't have a minute to themselves because their babies are *attached* to them. For several days after they hatch, the little fish stick to their parents' bodies. This discus never has to worry about where its babies are.

Photo Credits: Sharks

Wayne & Karen Brown: page 52
Al Grotell: page 44
David Hall: page 37
Richard Hermann: page 51
Marty Snyderman: pages 33, 48, 51, 52
Don Flescher/American Fisheries Society: page 35
Gotshall/American Fisheries Society: pages 50
Harold W. Pratt/Biological Photo Services: page 49
David J. Wrobel/Biological Photo Services: pages 35, 40
Doug Perrine/DRK: pages 33, 39, 45-47, 53
Rosemary Chastney/Images Unlimited: page 35
Al Giddings/Images Unlimited: page 32
Tom Campbell/Innerspace Visions: page 49
Mark Conlin/Innerspace Visions: pages 41, 53
David B. Fleetham/Innerspace Visions: page 45
Rudie Kuiter/Innerspace Visions: pages 44, 45, 50
Gwen Lowe/Innerspace Visions: pages 32, 44
Nigel Marsh/Innerspace Visions: page 41
Scott Michael/Innerspace Visions: page 51
Amos Nachoum/Innerspace Visions: page 46
Michael Nolan/Innerspace Visions: page 34
Doug Perrine/Innerspace Visions: pages 34, 37-41, 50, 52
Jeff Rotman/Innerspace Visions: page 52
Ron & Valerie Taylor/Innerspace Visions: page 39
Norbert Wu/Innerspace Visions: pages 40, 45
Flip Nicklin/Minden Pictures: pages 33, 36
Jim Watt/Pacific Stock: page 49
Stephen Frink/WaterHouse: pages 36, 47
Robert Jureit/WaterHouse: page 37
Marty Snyderman/WaterHouse: page 53
Ron & Valerie Taylor/WaterHouse: pages 37, 39, 47
Norbert Wu: pages 32, 33, 38, 47, 52, 53
Bruce Rasner/Norbert Wu: page 48

Illustrations
Robin Lee Makowski: pages 42, 43, 45

SHARKS

SHARK!

Terrifying, magnificent, mysterious—sharks are masters of the sea. They're real survivors, built so well that in the last 150 million years, they've had very little need to change, or *evolve*. And, in some form or another, they've been around for about 400 million years. Even before dinosaurs roamed the land, sharks ruled the oceans.

Pygmy shark

FAMILY MATTERS

Sharks belong to the group of fish known scientifically as *elasmobranchs* (e-LAS-ma-branks)—a big family. There are over 350 species, and they are very different from one another. Some are large, but most are fairly small. In fact, only 39 species are over 10 feet long. The largest is the whale shark (as big as a whale), and the smallest is the six-inch spined pygmy shark.

TELLTALE TEETH

How do we know there were ancient sharks? Their teeth have survived. Teeth are the best clues to shark evolution that we have. Although entire bodies of some sharks were found in the 19th century, usually it's the teeth, or even the scales, that have been preserved. Fossil teeth tell us about sharks that existed millions of years ago—and where the oceans used to be.

People used to believe that sharks never sleep. That's not true. Scientists have observed more and more sharks taking time out to rest on the bottom of the ocean. Nurse sharks sleep in piles of up to 40 members.

Whale shark

SENIOR CITIZEN

No one knows how long a shark lives. For example, scientists think the spiny dogfish shark may live for 30 years or for 100. To make a better guess, scientists now tag sharks in the wild and mark their spine with a chemical. The bones of a shark's spine have growth rings, just like a tree, which form through time. Scientists can later count the rings formed since the marking and guess a shark's age.

Bull shark

MEAT EATERS ▼

Almost all sharks are *carnivores*, or meat-eating animals. They eat other fish, even other sharks, and sea mammals like dolphins and seals. Some feed at the surface on *plankton*—a mixture of plants and shrimp-like creatures. Then, there are the bottom-dwelling sharks, which feed on *crustaceans* (such as crabs) and *mollusks* (such as clams), crunching them with specialized teeth.

A blue shark feeding on mackerel.

WORLD ▲ TRAVELERS

Sharks live all over the ocean, in cold to temperate waters—usually cooler than 90° F. Some live in shallow waters, while others live in the deep and on the ocean floor. Some, like the blue shark, *migrate*, or travel, thousands of miles. And some species, the bull shark in particular, can even swim from saltwater into freshwater. Bull sharks have been found in the Mississippi River.

BUILT TO LAST

Sharks used to be called "living fossils" because they seemed so primitive. However, the more scientists study sharks, the more they believe sharks are complex animals. In fact, sharks may be one of nature's best designs.

BONELESS

Most fish have skeletons of bone and are called bony fishes. A shark skeleton is different. It's made of *cartilage*—the same kind of material as the human ear and nose. Shark cartilage is not as hard as bone, but it is tough and flexible.

HANDS OFF ▲

The skin of most fish has scales, but shark scales are different. Called *denticles*, shark scales are constructed like teeth—very hard, sharp teeth. Shark skin is like a spiky suit of armor. You can be injured just by touching a shark.

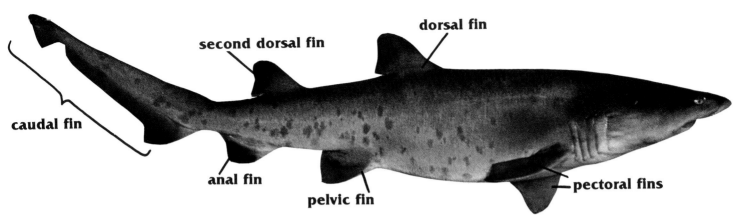

second dorsal fin

dorsal fin

caudal fin

anal fin

pelvic fin

pectoral fins

CRUISERS

A shark swims like no other fish. It doesn't flap and wiggle through the water. It glides. Its pectoral fins are stiff and are used for going up and down. The caudal fin is moved from side to side to propel the shark forward. Although some sharks can go fast enough to leap out of the water, sharks aren't built to swim fast all the time. Sharks are built to cruise slowly for long distances.

This shark has seven gills.

GILLS GALORE ▲

All fish use gills to breathe. Water passes into their mouth and out over the gills, which absorb the oxygen from the water into the fish's bloodstream. Unlike most fish, which have only a single pair of gill slits, sharks have five to seven pairs.

SINK OR SWIM

Most fish have a swim bladder that fills with air to keep them afloat when they're not swimming. A shark doesn't. It has to keep swimming to keep from sinking. But the shark has at least one flotation device—a big liver. The liver, which is sometimes a quarter of the shark's weight, contains oil. Since oil is lighter than water, it helps keep the shark afloat.

HOT BLOODS

Sharks are cold blooded, which means that their blood changes temperature as the water changes. But some sharks—the great white, the threshers, the salmon, the porbeagle, and two kinds of mako sharks—are known as "warm-bodied." They have a special heating system, so their blood is usually warmer than that of other sharks.

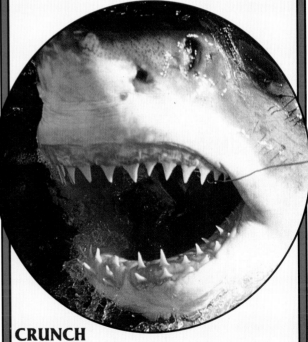

Great white shark

CRUNCH

The jaws of a shark are the most powerful on Earth. Both upper and lower jaws move. To bite, a shark strikes with its lower jaw first, then the upper. It flings its head from side to side to tear loose a piece of meat.

SUPERSHARP SENSES

A shark can hear, smell, and feel everything in the water—at great distances. With these supersharp senses, the shark has an excellent design for hunting. A school of fish may be passing through, or a fish may be hurt. The shark knows the difference and it reacts quickly, zooming toward its prey with deadly accuracy.

SMART SHARK

Sharks are often thought of as "swimming noses"—that they only use their brain to smell out food. Some, however, are fairly smart and can learn. Generally, the more active, fast-moving sharks have brains that are more complex than those of slower, bottom-dwelling sharks.

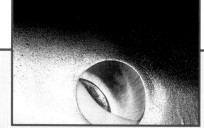

The nictitating membrane of a blue shark partially covering the eye.

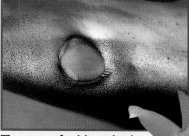

The eye of a blue shark completely covered by the nictitating membrane.

BLINK

Most fish have no eyelids, but some sharks have three—an upper, a lower, and a second lower lid. This second lower lid, called a *nictitating membrane*, can clamp shut and protect the whole eye in dangerous situations—like when the shark feeds.

GOOD VIBRATIONS

A shark can hear movement in the water, but it can also feel the vibrations by using its *lateral line*. This is a line of canals that runs from head to tail, linked to the surface of the shark by pores. Each canal is filled with seawater and contains special sensory cells with hairlike projections. These hairs move with vibrations in the water and then send messages to the shark's brain.

SWIMMING NOSE

Sharks do have a good sense of smell. In that sense, they *are* swimming noses! Two-thirds of a shark's brain controls its sense of smell. The two nostrils on a shark's snout are full of cells that detect odors in the water. In one experiment, sharks smelled a small bit of tuna from 75 feet away—smelling one-part tuna juice to a million-and-a-half parts water.

Blue shark

Lemon shark

Some sharks, like this lemon shark, have a vertically slit pupil.

NIGHT SIGHT

What do cats and sharks have in common? Their eyes. Both have eyes with a mirror-like layer that reflects light. This physical trait allows them to see better in the dark. So, whether in clear water or murky seas, a shark can still hunt.

▼ ELECTRIC DIRECTION

All creatures have an electrical field. A shark "feels" this electrical activity with sensory organs called *ampullae of Lorenzini*. Leading to these organs are many pores, sometimes over 1,500 on the shark's head. Using its ampullae, a shark can find flat fish hiding under the sand. Because the Earth, too, has a magnetic field, it is thought that sharks may use this sense as a compass as well.

37

A BITE TO EAT

The mako shark has long, narrow, pointed teeth.

Rows of serrated, or saw-like, teeth in the jaw of a tiger shark.

Think of sharks and you think of sharp, pointed teeth. But there are many different kinds of teeth. Shark teeth are so unique that scientists can identify sharks by them—or by the bite they leave behind.

DENTAL PLAN

Sharks have a lifetime supply of teeth—rows and rows set in soft tissue. An adult probably goes through 7 to 12 sets in one year. Each time a tooth is lost, by biting or through aging, a new tooth moves forward and takes its place. Some sharks, like the cookiecutter, swallow whole sets of teeth at one time when eating.

IN SHAPE FOR EATING ▲

Sharks do not chew. They swallow things whole or in big pieces. Some use their teeth like a fork and knife—they have pointed teeth in the lower jaw to puncture prey, and *serrated* teeth in the top to saw away at meat. But teeth vary from shark to shark, because the shape of a shark's tooth is related to the type of food it eats and the way it hunts.

A great white tooth on top of a Megalodon tooth.

TOOTH TALE

Scientists have found the teeth of a creature they call the Megalodon, an ancestor of the great white shark. It lived about 12,000 years ago, and it was *huge*. Its teeth were six inches long—more than twice the size of a great white's teeth.

ON THE MENU

Eating to survive is the name of the game in the ocean, and sharks are the champs. Some eat plankton, and some eat mollusks and crustaceans (like snails and shrimp) at the bottom of the ocean. Then there are those that eat larger prey, such as seals, turtles, seagulls, and dolphins.

▲ A shark feeding on a turtle.

▲ The Port Jackson shark has sharp teeth in front for puncturing, and large molars in back for crunching the shells of mollusks.

Tiger shark

SHARK EAT SHARK

Sharks don't just eat other sea creatures. They also eat each other. Once, a tiger shark was caught with a bull shark in its stomach. In the bull shark's belly, scientists found a blacktip shark. And the blacktip's stomach revealed a dogfish shark!

FEEDING FRENZY

Normally, sharks dine alone. But sometimes they have a vicious party—a feeding frenzy. One feeding shark may attract others. Racing to the scene, they slash at the prey and bite wildly at anything that gets in their way—even each other. Then, it's over as quickly as it began.

SPECIAL DELIVERY

There are three ways that sharks begin life. They hatch from eggs outside their mother's body, the way chickens do. They hatch from eggs within the mother and are then born. Or, like people, their mother gives birth to them. Sharks have from 1 to 100 babies at a time, depending on the way they reproduce. The ones that give birth to a fully developed shark have fewer babies at a time than sharks that lay eggs outside their body.

▲
A lemon shark is born!

BORN AT LAST

Sharks that are born, instead of hatched, grow inside the mother in much the same way human babies do. However, it can take sharks longer than nine months to finish developing. The spiny dogfish is pregnant for almost two years with her pups.

◄ Dogfish shark embryo

▲ The newborn lemon shark and mother.

Cat shark egg cases

THAT'S AN EGG?

Shark eggs are not "egg-shaped" like chicken eggs. They are tough, leathery, and rectangular, or shaped like spirals and screws. As the baby shark develops inside this *egg case*, it feeds on the yolk part like chickens do. In 8 to 14 months, a shark is fully developed right down to its teeth.

▶
Cat shark embryo and yolk

(1)

(2)

(3)

Full-grown
sandtiger shark

CANNIBAL BABY▲

A female sandtiger shark carries eggs that hatch inside its body. It produces many eggs, but the first to hatch is likely to be the only one born. This baby eats its underdeveloped brothers and sisters. That's how it grows—and grows. When it's born, the baby is about 40% the size of its mother—that's almost half.

THE GOOD MOTHER

Although sharks do not care for their babies after they have come into the world, mothers will search out safe places, called *nurseries*, where they can lay eggs or give

A pile of the spiral-shaped egg cases of the Port Jackson shark.

birth. The Port Jackson shark mother seems especially attentive to finding a safe place for her eggs. Scientists think that she carries them around in her mouth after laying them, looking for a reef crevice in which to lodge them for safe hatching.

A swell shark emerges from its egg case and swims off to live on its own (1-4).

(4)

TOUGH PUPS

A baby shark is called a *pup*, but it doesn't lead a dog's life. Its mother doesn't feed it or give it hunting lessons. In fact, grown sharks are happy to make a meal of tender babies. To survive, many young sharks go close to shore to grow up on their own. There are small fish to feed on there and no large sharks around.

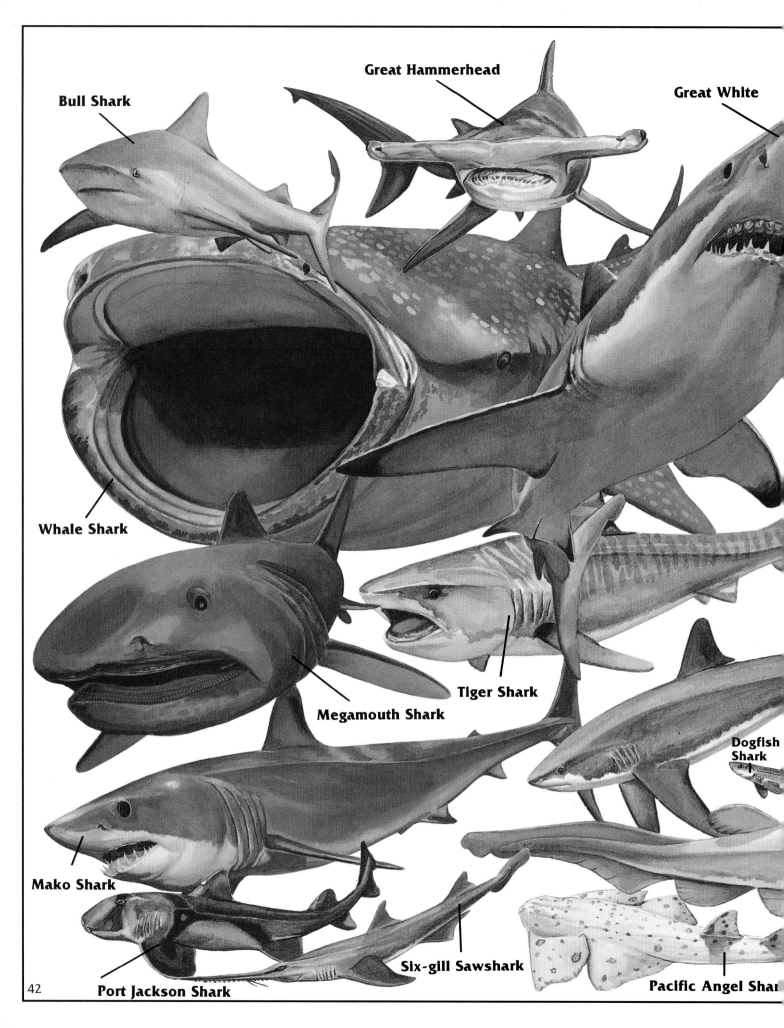

Great Hammerhead

Great White

Bull Shark

Whale Shark

Megamouth Shark

Tiger Shark

Dogfish Shark

Mako Shark

Six-gill Sawshark

Pacific Angel Shark

Port Jackson Shark

42

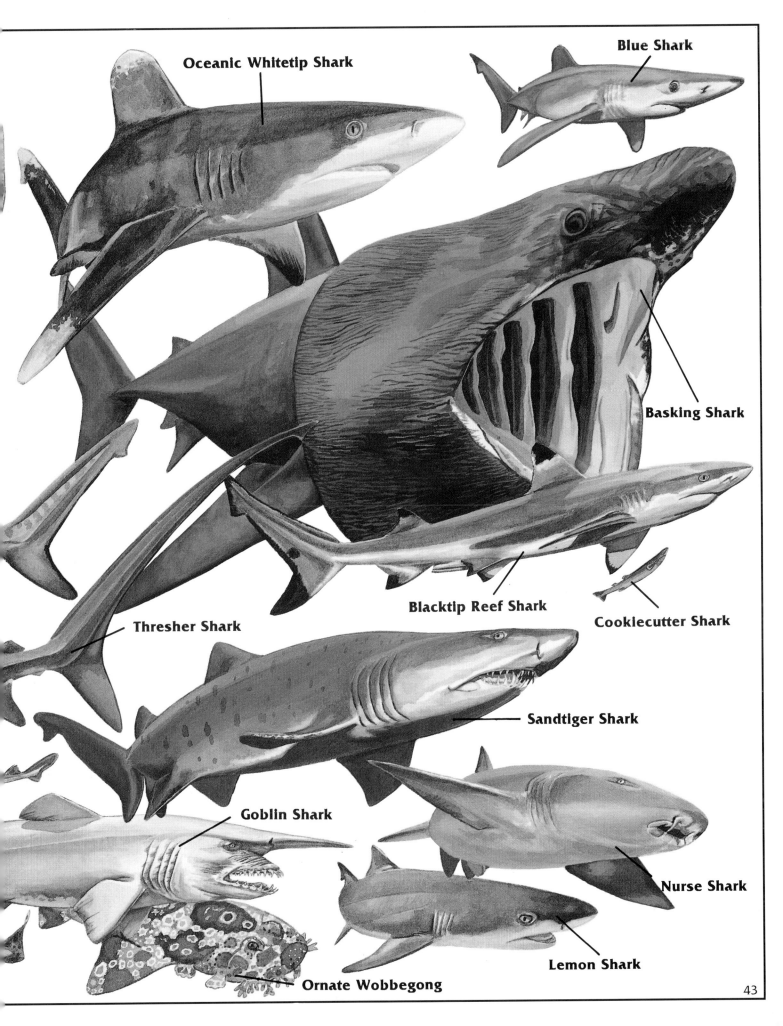

Oceanic Whitetip Shark

Blue Shark

Basking Shark

Blacktip Reef Shark

Cookiecutter Shark

Thresher Shark

Sandtiger Shark

Goblin Shark

Nurse Shark

Lemon Shark

Ornate Wobbegong

43

WEIRD RELATIONS

All sharks are hard to get to know. They have such a large living space that often they can't be found. Some sharks are rarely seen at all, and some are so weird to look at that, when you see them, you may not think they're sharks. In fact, one thing that is easy to see is how different sharks are—especially in the way they look.

Scalloped hammerheads are known to school when they migrate (above).

▲Smooth hammerhead

HAMMER JAMMER ▲

Having eyes and nostrils sometimes a yard apart, a hammerhead shark is able to sample a wide range of water at one time, sniffing out food as it swings its head from left to right. And, as if one weird head were not enough, there are many types of hammerheads.

◀ ANCIENT EATER

The frilled shark is often called "primitive" because it closely resembles some extinct species—some types of sharks that have disappeared from the Earth. The frilled shark has a slithery, snakelike body and 300 teeth set in 27 rows.

◀ HUNTING TAIL

The thresher shark has a 10-foot tail— that's about half as long as its body. This shark herds small fish together and hits them—whack—with its tail. Threshers are thought to be harmless to humans, but there is a story about one fisherman in the Atlantic who lost his head when swiped by a thresher's tail.

44

▼ COOL CATS

Cat sharks live mostly in deep waters and are rarely seen. They are one of the largest shark groups and live all over the ocean. But very little is known about them.

▲ SPOOKY

Maybe it's the strangest-looking shark of all, and, because it lives in deep water, it's almost never seen! Until found off the coast of Japan in 1898, the goblin shark was believed to be extinct for 100 million years.

Cookiecutter shark

IN THE TANK ▲

Some sharks are so gentle, they can be kept in aquariums. The zebra shark, also known as the leopard shark, is very gentle. It's spotted like a leopard, and its tail is half its length.

A dolphin with a cookiecutter wound.

CRUNCH

The cookiecutter shark is a 20-inch-long creature that feeds on whales and dolphins. With its circular set of teeth, the cookiecutter chomps a perfectly round hole out of its victim. Its teeth are so sharp, it has damaged rubber-covered parts of submarines.

Zebra bullhead shark

OLD TIMER ▲

Bullhead sharks are the oldest unchanged sharks. Fossils of them have been found in rocks 200 million years old.

DANGER!

Here's the nightmare: You see a fin and then a giant shark grabs you and crushes you with its teeth. Wake up! It's probably a dream. Here are the facts. Worldwide, fewer than 100 people are attacked in an average year by sharks. Some of these cases are provoked attacks, where the shark is caught, trapped, speared, or somehow bothered by people.

The most dangerous shark, the great white is known to chase down boats and attack them until they sink.

THE GREATEST

The great white shark is one of the largest, most deadly predators. Credited with more attacks on humans than any other shark, it grows to be about 11 1/2 feet and 7,000 pounds. Twenty-foot great whites have also been reported! It's the only shark that will lift its head above water.

TIGER OF THE SEA

The tiger shark is second only to the great white in the number of attacks on people. There is very little in the sea that the tiger shark doesn't eat. Some have been found with a few weird objects in their bellies—such as boat cushions, unopened cans of salmon, an alarm clock, tar paper, and a keg of nails! ▶

The great hammerhead is sometimes found in water only 3-feet deep.

Mako shark

HAMMER HORROR

Seeing a hammerhead in the water might be enough to scare a swimmer to death, but scientists don't think that hammerheads are man-eaters. However, they consider a few kinds, like the great hammerhead and the smooth hammerhead, to be potentially dangerous because of their size.

KNACK FOR ATTACK

About 27 kinds of sharks are known to have attacked humans, and there are others considered dangerous. Shark attacks usually occur where there are a lot of people—in fairly warm, waist-deep water. It's possible that all the vibrations in the water resemble those of a wounded fish—a favorite shark meal. Attacks also occur where people are fishing.

SWORD SWALLOWER

The mako is powerful and thought to be dangerous. It is the fastest shark of all, clocked at 43 miles per hour. It is known to leap out of water—sometimes into boats! Also, the mako seems to have very little fear. A large, 730-pound mako was once caught with a 120-pound swordfish in its stomach—sword and all!

Bull shark

▲ BRUTAL BULL

The bull shark doesn't look as frightening as the great white, but it is in some ways more dangerous—certainly in the tropics. Listed as the third-most dangerous man-eater, the bull shark swims in places that people do—in salt water and fresh water.

◀ The blacktip reef shark is dangerous.

NO-TEAR WEAR

People have tried over and over again to come up with chemical products and special diving suits that will repel sharks. One kind of suit found to help protect divers against bites is made of steel mesh.

Tiger shark

A diver wearing a steel-mesh suit while feeding a shark.

HUGE AND HARMLESS

Sharks are not always fierce and aggressive. Some sharks are harmless. And, strangely enough, the most harmless sharks are huge. These two characteristics, which do not seem to go together, belong to the basking shark, whale shark, and megamouth shark. They are the gentle giants of the shark family.

WHALE SHARK

The whale shark is the biggest fish in the world. Only about 100 have ever been seen. One captured near Pakistan in 1949 measured 41 1/2 feet long and was estimated to weigh 33,000 pounds.

ALL ABOARD

Believe it or not, whale sharks are so harmless, they let divers hold on to their fins for a ride. One diver says the feeling is like clinging to an underwater freight train. When whale sharks become tired of their human passengers, they dive deep into the sea.

◀ BIG SURPRISE

About 20 years ago, a navy ship off Hawaii accidentally hauled in a type of shark that had never before been discovered. It weighed over 6,000 pounds. Scientists gave it a name to fit its face: megamouth. It was another harmless, giant shark.

▲ SUNBATHERS

A basking shark can usually grow to be 30 feet long and 8,000 pounds. This fish is a mammoth sunbather. Its name comes from its habit of lying motionless in surface waters with its back above the surface and its nose and fins sticking out—as if it were "basking" in the sun.

▼ THROAT STRAIN

These huge, plankton-eating sharks feed by keeping their mouth open while swimming forward. Whatever comes in is strained from the water by *gill rakers* at the back of their throat. After awhile they swallow their catch. A cruising basking shark can strain about 2,000 gallons of water an hour.

A whale shark feeding.

▼ MINI-FOOD

Plankton is the diet of these big sharks. *Copepods*—barely visible lobster and shrimp-like creatures—are a large part of plankton. Scientists figure that sharks eat about 1% of their body's weight each day. For an 8,000-pound basking shark, that's a lot of plankton.

Copepods

The whale shark—the biggest fish in the world.

THE DEEP

What's more mysterious than the deep blue sea? The sharks that live there. There are many different types of bottom-dwelling sharks, and a few of them are really strange-looking. Some eat mussels, clams, and snails. Others prey on the swimming creatures that share their home at the bottom of the ocean.

A nurse shark exploring a reef. ▼

DEVILISH ANGEL

It's flat like its relative, the skate, but it swims like a shark, powered by its oar-like tail fin. It is a shark, an angel shark, but it's not an angel! Although the angel lounges motionless on the bottom, it has a swift and deadly bite, having sharp, dagger-like teeth for impaling fish and crustaceans. Fishermen who have tangled with it call it the "sand devil."

◄ SAWTOOTH

Here's one shark with teeth on the outside of its mouth. It's the sawshark. It has a long, flat, blade-like snout with teeth on either side, like a saw. Unborn sawsharks keep their teeth folded back until birth, protecting the mothers who carry them inside their body.

The face of a horn shark.

HORN BACK ▲

This strange-looking bottom dweller, called the horn shark, can be found in shallow waters, too. Why is it called the horn shark? If you look closely at its dorsal fin, you can see a little horn at the front. People make jewelry out of these pretty fin spines.

Chain dogfish shark

KILLER CARPET

To lie in wait on the ocean floor is the carpet shark's hunting plan. And no wonder! Carpet sharks have markings that blend in with the sand and a head that looks like a mop of weeds. No one sees it! Any fish that comes by is quickly snatched.

This creature, a kind of carpet shark called a Wobbegong (WOB-e-gong), is found in waters around Australia and the Far East.

A DOG OF A FISH

Spiny dogfish, smooth dogfish, spotted dogfish, chain dogfish—dogfish sharks are a large, varied family and their names prove it. In the 1400's, people with little knowledge of the sea gave them the "dog" tag. They called the sharks sea dogs or dog fish simply because these sharks have sharp teeth.

HOW SWELL! ▼

The swell shark is a lazy-bones, deep-bottom fish. It is so sluggish that it's called "sleepy Joe." But when threatened, this shark swells up by gulping air, until the center of its body is nearly twice its normal size. Why? Perhaps for defense, or to wedge itself into a tight hiding place. Both are swell ideas!

51

SHARKS AND PEOPLE

The shark is often used as a symbol for things that are frightening or dangerous. But, through studying them, scientists have learned enough about sharks not to think of them simply as killing machines. In fact, people are more dangerous to sharks than sharks are to people. We hunt them, pollute their water, and cause them injury, sometimes depleting whole populations.

Many sharks, like this dogfish, get caught in people's fishing nets and die. ◄

The jaw of this blue shark was probably torn by a fishing line or net, which are known to injure sharks and other sea creatures.

TREASURED TEETH
Shark teeth have been treasured for hundreds of years. People used to use fossilized teeth as charms to ward off evil and protect against poisoning. Pacific Islanders used shark teeth to make weapons (left). Today, people make jewelry out of shark teeth.

SKIN DEEP
People have hunted sharks for their skin for centuries. Sharkskin is 100% stronger than cowhide. It's used like any other leather, to make products such as shoes, belts, and purses.

MAIN COURSE

Shark steak or shark's fin soup on the menu? It's true. Soup is made from the fibers within a shark's fins, and shark meat is cooked like any other fish. In the United States, mako is sold all over. But in many countries shark steak may appear on the menu under a different name. The piked dogfish is known as "rock salmon" in Britain and as "flake" in Australia.

A mako shark caught by a fisherman.

Unfortunately, some fishermen cut the fins off a shark for shark's fin soup, then throw the rest of the shark, still alive, back in the water to die.

TO YOUR HEALTH

Shark's livers were an important source of vitamin A until the 1950's, when scientists learned how to make this vitamin. Now, sharks are important to human health in other ways: Shark cartilage contains a chemical that is used to make skin for burn victims; and shark corneas have been successfully transplanted into human eyes.

◀ To study aging, these scientists are injecting a tiger shark with medicine that will mark the growth rings in its backbone.

▼ These scientists are working on a project to capture, test, and tag sharks.

STUDY BUDDY

Scientists also study sharks just to find out more about them, but it's not easy. When you can locate them, in the vast open sea, they're not always doing the things that you want to find out about, such as giving birth, schooling, or sleeping. But scientists have come up with procedures, like tagging and tracking, to get to know sharks better.

Here, a scientist studies the flow of water through a nurse shark's breathing system.▼

Scientific Consultant:
Paul Sweet
American Museum of Natural History

PENGUINS

WHAT A BIRD!

You may know them by their waddle and their black and white feathers. But penguins are so much more! All these tough birds are super swimmers. Some live in the bitter cold, as far south as Antarctica, where ice presents another fun way to travel.

OLD BIRD
Penguins are an ancient bird family. Fossils 50 to 60 million years old have been found on the coasts of New Zealand and Australia.

WATER WAYS
Ancestors of penguins were probably able to fly. But today's penguins fly only underwater. Some spend as much as 75 percent of their time in the ocean, where they make very deep dives to find food.

◀ Penguins don't fly, but they can leap!

56

PERFECT PENGUIN

Go to the zoo and you'll most likely see Adélie (uh-DAY-lee) Penguins. There are more Adélies than any other kind of penguin in captivity. Adélies are medium-sized—about 10 pounds and 2¹/₂ feet tall. Wearing a "tuxedo," they're everybody's idea of what a penguin looks like. But nature has created different kinds of penguins.

FUNNY FELLOWS ▲

Penguins seem a little clumsy when they walk. That's because their legs are placed far back on their body. They have to stand up straight or they'll fall over. Their walk may look awkward and comical—but it gets them where they're going.

PENGUIN PARTIES

Penguins have very active social lives. Some species gather in huge, noisy groups to find mates and breed. These places, called "rookeries," are penguin cities, filled with thousands upon thousands of birds.

NAME THAT BIRD

Penguins have wonderful names. The King and Emperor are the largest. The Chinstrap is named for its special markings. The Rockhopper's name comes from its fancy footwork (shown below) in bouncing from rock to rock.

◀ The Rockhopper Penguin

57

SO DIFFERENT!

Will the real penguin please stand up? There are 17 species of penguins, and no two are exactly alike. Some have orange head tufts that look like crazy eyebrows. Some have brushy tails. Some are aggressive. Others are mild-mannered.

An Emperor Penguin and chick

HEAVYWEIGHTS

Three and a half feet and over 60 pounds is a lot of bird. That's the Emperor, the largest of all. The King Penguin is the next heaviest at about 35 pounds. With lovely orange or yellow patches around their ears, and brilliant orange around their neck, the Kings are very handsome birds.

The King Penguin

PINT-SIZED PENGUIN

The shy Little Penguin is so delicate, it has been called the Fairy Penguin. It grows to only a foot and a half, weighs under three pounds, and is the smallest of all penguins.

FEATHERED FRIENDS

The Macaroni Penguin has a "crest" of orange and yellow feathers. It gets its name from a fancy hairstyle that was popular among young men in England during the late 18th and early 19th centuries.

LOUDMOUTH

The Chinstrap is one of the brush-tailed penguins, which have long tails that sweep behind them. The Chinstrap stands a little over two feet tall and has a black stripe across its chin. It also has an ear-splitting call.

DONKEY CALL

A penguin that looks like it's been standing in the mud is the Black-footed Penguin. Its less lovely name is the Jackass Penguin because it makes a loud bray-ing noise like a donkey.

YELLOW-EYED

The Yellow-eyed is one of the tallest penguins. A bit different from the black-and-white variety of penguins, the Yellow-eyed has a slate-blue back, white undersides, and striking yellow eyes.

JUMPING GENTOO

A white band that goes from eye to eye is the mark of the Gentoo Penguin. This 14-pound bird, sometimes called the Johnny Penguin, runs, jumps, and even slides on its belly on sand.

59

BOLD LIVING

Penguins live only below the equator. Some come ashore on Antarctica, frigid home of the South Pole. But others do not live in cold places. They are found on the coasts and islands of South America, Africa, Australia, and New Zealand.

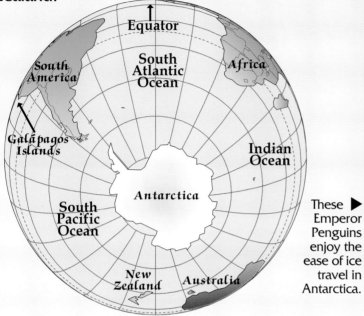

These ► Emperor Penguins enjoy the ease of ice travel in Antarctica.

ICE ISLAND

Antarctica, covered by a sheet of ice nearly a mile thick, is one of the coldest places on Earth. This continent is the breeding ground of the Adélie, Emperor, Chinstrap, and Gentoo penguins. But the Emperor is the only penguin that spends the winter there.

Adélies in a snowstorm.

▲ BIRD-WATCHING

The first time Europeans set eyes on a penguin was when explorer Vasco da Gama sailed down the coast of Africa in 1499. One surprised sailor reported that he saw birds that couldn't fly, and which made a sound like a mule. Almost 500 years later, the Black-footed Penguin is still there, living on the coasts and small islands around the southern tip of Africa.

60

HOMEBODIES ▼

The coasts of New Zealand, Australia, and some surrounding islands are the homes of Little Penguins. These birds don't migrate like some other penguins. They travel only between their nest and the sea, about a third of a mile. It's a short but risky trip, threatened by the likes of cats, dogs, weasels, and even cars.

NAMESAKE ▼

Magellanic Penguins have a name from the history books. When Ferdinand Magellan, the Portuguese explorer, led the first expedition around the world in 1519, he sailed around the tip of South America. That's where the Magellanics live, on both the Pacific and Atlantic coasts.

HOT AND COLD

Galapagos Penguins make their nests on the Galapagos Islands, off the coast of South America. That's nearly on the equator, a very hot spot! But the ocean there is cold, fed by a current flowing from the icy Antarctic— and filled with the foods that penguins like to eat.

▼ Galapagos Penguins share their home with another ocean-goer— the marine iguana.

WARM BODIES

Penguins are warm-blooded creatures, just like people. Their normal body temperature is 100 to 102°F. Ours is 98.6°F. How do they stay warm in icy waters? Layers of insulation. Under their skin they have fat, known as blubber. Covering the skin are fluffy feathers, called *down*, and a tightly packed layer of outer feathers, which seals in warmth.

CUDDLE HUDDLE ▲

Emperor penguins have the coldest breeding grounds—in Antarctica. They incubate their eggs in extreme weather, standing motionless on the ice. Sometimes one body just doesn't create enough heat. So they form a tight huddle. That's as many as 6,000 penguins squeezing shoulder to shoulder!

◀ BONE BONUS

Normally, birds have light, hollow bones that make flight easier. But penguins have heavy, solid bones that suit their way of life in the water. The weight lets them get their body underwater—where they can use their powerful flippers to swim.

SUPER FEET

There's more to penguins than feathers. Look at their feet. On land, penguins can walk, run, and hop. At sea, they use their webbed feet as rudders for steering.

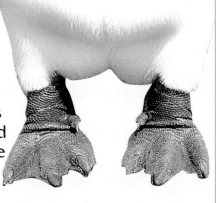

◀ FEATHER CARE ▶

A penguin's feathers are slick and dense. One square inch of penguin is covered with about 70 feathers, all overlapping like fish scales or shingles on a roof. Penguins *preen* their feathers, applying oil from an oil gland. The overlapping feathers and the oil create a waterproof, windproof suit.

◀ Two bills are better than one, so these Macaroni Penguins seem to think.

This ▶ Gentoo gets its feathers ready for the water by preening.

▼ AIR WAYS

Too hot or too cold, both are problems for penguins. In warm places, such as the Galapagos Islands, penguins need to cool off. Feather fluffing is the answer. Penguins can lift their feathers and keep them up, so air can cool their skin. They also stick out their winglike flippers to help heat escape.

COLOR COATED

Color counts when a penguin is trying to keep warm. Black absorbs heat, and white reflects heat. A chilly penguin turns its black back to the sun and absorbs the warmth. A penguin in danger of overheating turns its white chest to the sun to reflect light.

This Galapagos Penguin stretches out its flippers to cool off.

MADE TO MOLT ▼

Feathers don't last forever. Most birds replace them by *molting,* shedding old feathers and growing new ones. But penguins need their feathers in the icy sea. They molt all at once, and during that time—as long as a month—they stay out of the water.

WATER WINGS

A penguin is a bird that "flies" underwater. Unlike other birds, penguins have short stiff paddlelike wings called flippers. Underwater, they propel themselves forward in a flying motion, flapping their wings about two times a second, just as other birds do in the air.

SHAPED TO SWIM ▲

Look at a penguin underwater and think of a submarine or torpedo. With this sleek streamlined body, penguins can slice through water like a seal or dolphin. Their average swimming speed is 15 miles per hour.

▲ Rockhoppers make spectacular leaps.

DEEP DIVERS

No bird can dive like a penguin. A penguin will drop 70 feet just to grab a meal. Penguins are known to stay underwater for up to 18 minutes. Emperor Penguins have been observed 1200 feet below the surface of the water—an amazing and probably rare dive.

These ▶ Adélies are ready to dive in!

LEAPING FOR AIR ▼

"Porpoising" is the penguin way of breathing while swimming. Penguins speed up underwater, shoot out above the surface, and breathe. Then they dive back under for another go-around.

◀ UP AND OVER

Going from water onto land is a simple task for penguins. They just waddle out. But when they face steep walls of ice, snow, or rock, they leap. They dive down and then swim up so rapidly that they shoot out of the water—as high as 6 feet—and land safely on their feet.

SPEED SLIDE

To move faster on ice, penguins *toboggan.* They lie belly-down on the ground, push with their feet and flippers, and glide like a person on a sled. This speeds them up from two or three miles an hour walking, to eight miles an hour tobogganing.

SEAFOOD

For penguins, fish is always on the menu. They also eat krill, crustaceans, and squid. Krill are tiny shrimplike animals found in enormous numbers. The world's penguin population eats tons of krill every day. In Antarctica, during mating season when millions of penguins gather, they may eat half of the Antarctic Ocean's available food.

FISHING GEAR ▼

For snapping up a meal, penguins have fishing equipment—a sharp bill with hooks that fit together. Their tongue is equipped with backwards-facing bristles that grab the wiggling prey and thrust it down the throat.

◄ Krill

PICKY PENGUINS

Just like people, penguins have food preferences. The Adélies' favorite is krill. Magellanics go for squid, and Black-footed Penguins want fish and more fish. Of course, where they live, how deep they dive, and what swims by has a lot to do with what each penguin eats.

SALTSHAKER ▼

Surrounded by saltwater, penguins can't get fresh water to drink. So their body "makes" fresh water for them. Penguins have a gland that removes the salt from the water and releases it through grooves in their bill.

▼ MOUTH TO MOUTH

Food for chicks comes straight from a parent's mouth. The adults return with undigested food stored in their *crop,* a special pouch in the throat. A chick fits its bill inside the adult's mouth to receive the food. An Emperor parent may deliver seven pounds of food at a time to its chick.

BODY STORAGE

An Emperor Penguin's large body is built to store food. During the whole breeding period they eat nothing. It is not until the egg is laid that one parent leaves for the sea to eat. An Emperor male, who goes without food longer than any other penguin—for 15 weeks or more in -40°F weather—loses nearly half his body weight. When he does eat, the Emperor dad may consume 30 pounds of food at one time.

THE MATING GAME

In the mating season, all penguins head for land. Each species has its own territory, and some are very far from their ocean homes. The Adélies nest in the spring, which begins in October in Antarctica. But the land is still surrounded by sea ice. To reach their rookery, the penguins trudge across the ice—for as much as 60 miles! ▶

◀ CHILLY WINTER
Emperor Penguins start breeding in the winter, which begins in March. There is no sun at that time. The penguins stay on the grim ice for six months, until their chicks are ready to be on their own when summer arrives.

SHOW-OFFS ▶
A male penguin has a walk that gets females to follow him. It's called a "display" or "advertisement walk." The King Penguin, with his spectacular orange neck markings, is the best on the block. He struts and turns his head from side to side so the female can see just how handsome he is.

LOVE CALL
There is high drama in the rookeries when mating begins. Each male must attract a female, and they do it by "calling." They stand with their back arched, head raised, and wings outstretched, and raise a wild trumpeting cry.

TUNE FOR TWO

All penguin pairs "sing" a duet as part of their display, and it's not just for entertainment. They learn to recognize each other's voice. That's very important because there are thousands of look-alikes in a rookery.

▼ YOU'RE MINE!

When a male and female become a pair, they cement the bond in a "mutual display." The two penguins, depending on the species, may raise their heads, touch necks, vibrate their flippers, or slap each other on the back.

PENGUIN PAIRS

Most penguins stick to the same partner. One theory for this behavior is that most return to their old territory and meet up automatically. But some scientists believe that penguins recognize each other by voice and sight, even after a year.

NEST, SWEET NEST

To build a nest, to find a mate, and to breed—that is the life's work of a penguin. All species are similar in these activities, but they are different, too. Just look at their nests!

▲ GHOSTLY GROUND

On the eastern coast of Argentina, there is an eerie noise that comes from holes in the ground, inspiring legends of ghosts and even devils. The sound comes from penguins—thousands of Magellanics, whose dug-in burrows form huge underground cities.

Black-footed Penguins dig burrows, too, ▶ but will also build nests above ground, using vegetation, feathers, or stones.

A Rockhopper and its egg.

BOUNCING BIRDS

Rockhoppers build nests on steep rocky areas. They get there by jumping. With both feet held together, they bounce 4 to 5 feet from one ledge to another. Macaroni Penguins build their nests on steep, rough ground, too. Sometimes they build on lava flows, rock slopes, and in caves.

▲ Nesting Macaroni mates.

PRECIOUS STONES ▶

Stones are like diamonds to Adélies. Stones are the only material they have to build their nests on Antarctica. Sometimes the right-sized rocks are in short supply. So every Adélie watches its stones, or a neighbor will steal them!

◀ MALE DUTY

As soon as eggs are laid, the female heads for the sea to find food. The male stays with the eggs. By the time the Adélie female returns, the males haven't eaten for about two weeks. Then it's his turn to eat while she stays with the egg.

TAKING TURNS ▶

Gentoos hollow a nest in the ground and line it with grass. Then the male and female take turns keeping the egg warm against their *brood patch,* a featherless area on the belly.

FOOTHOLD

King Penguins have a territory rather than a nest. They incubate an egg standing up, and the spot where they stand is theirs. The sea is close to their colony, so parents eat and return often.

LIVING TOGETHER

Gather thousands of penguins together and what have you got? A rookery. Large rookeries can cover miles. But each pair of penguins gets only about one square yard of space to build a nest. It's crowded and noisy, but it's home.

▼ VOICES CARRY

Penguins get along in these huge throngs by "calling"—a cross between trumpets blaring and donkeys braying. Each species has its own unique call. Each penguin has its own particular sound. And they locate one another by voice. Shouting, they let each other know to "watch out" or "stay clear!"

In a rookery, it gets really crowded!

◄ King Penguins communicating.

72

◀ BODY LANGUAGE

Penguins communicate by gesture as well as by voice. They bump, paddle, and peck. They stare, bow, and crouch. Through sound and movement, they let others know their situation. They are male or female. They need a mate or don't. They want a nest or have one. They like each other or not.

SAFE CIRCLE ▼

For almost all animals, there is safety in numbers, especially when it comes to the young. When chicks are strong enough, both parents head for the sea. The chicks group together in a *creche,* or nursery, where they're less likely to be attacked by predators.

▼ Emperor chicks have to huddle to keep warm.

MA! IT'S ME! ▶

Ever get lost? Imagine looking for your parents among millions of others! But in the penguin world, chicks and parents recognize each other's calls and always find one another. Even while the chick is breaking out of its egg, it is calling so its parent will get to know its voice.

73

CHICK TIME

Male and female penguins really work together when it's time to build a nest, lay eggs, and raise chicks. The survival of their baby depends on their cooperation. It's a tough job for the chicks, too, just to grow up.

BABIES ON ICE ▼

Being born in Antarctica is like beginning life in a freezer. When they hatch, chicks are helpless and cold. They have soft down feathers instead of the sleek, waterproof coats of their parents. The Emperor chick must stand on a parent's feet, not touching the ice for the first two months of its life, or it will freeze.

▼ Emperor chick

▼ A Chinstrap parent and chicks.

ONE CHICK, OR TWO?

Penguins may lay two eggs, but sometimes only one survives. The Chinstrap usually lays two same-sized eggs. The eggs hatch on the same day, and the chicks are treated equally. But Gentoos lay two different-sized eggs, the larger one first. The smaller chick may not survive if there's not enough food for both.

◀ This newly hatched Gentoo chick enjoys a foot seat.

74

NEST REST

Chicks hatched in a nest will stay there for awhile. It is their period of *brooding,* a time when their parents still keep them warm and protected. A Rockhopper chick stays around its nest for about three weeks, but by ten weeks it has gone to sea.

King Penguin chicks form a creche after about three weeks, when they have a layer of thick brown down.

CHICK CLUB

Some chicks don't hang out in their nest until they're old enough to leave. They form a creche instead. When parents return from gathering food, the chicks break from their group and chase their parents down. Then the parents feed them.

TO BE A BIG BIRD

When chicks grow their adult feathers and are ready to go to sea, they are said to be *fledging.* King chicks stay in their creche for about nine months before they molt and leave. Afterward, they no longer depend on their parents.

A molting King Penguin chick.

75

PREYING ON PENGUINS

Penguins fall prey to many different predators, especially to leopard seals. The seals hide below the ice and wait for the penguins to jump into the sea. One leopard seal can eat 15 Adélie penguins in one day.

◀This seal is pursuing some Gentoo Penguins.

▼Penguins will jump over cracks in the ice to avoid leopard seals.

SAFETY SUIT

A black-and-white swimsuit means safety for a penguin. If a predator is below, looking up, it may not see the penguin's white underside because it would blend in with the light of the sky. If the enemy is above, looking down, it cannot see the penguin's black back against the ocean's dark depths.

FOOD THIEF

Sheathbills are pigeonlike birds in the Antarctic that attack when parents feed their chicks. The sheathbill alarms the penguins, causing the food to fall to the ground. The thief then grabs the prize, flies home, and feeds its own chicks.

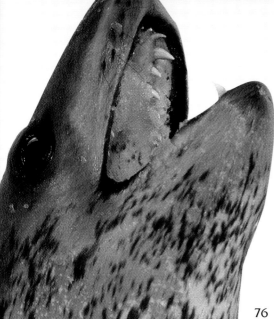

◀A leopard seal.

A penguin tries to protect its▶ egg from a sheathbill, which eats penguin eggs as well as penguin food.

▲ BODY SNATCHER

In the Antarctic, skuas swoop down and feed on penguin chicks. To avoid adult penguins, who could defend a chick, the skua may push and roll the little bird away from the rookery where it can more easily be attacked.

Penguins have to watch out for this sneaky blue-tongued lizard.

This sea eagle from Australia is a fierce predator of penguins.

HAZARDS AT HOME

The penguin enemy list is greater on land than at sea. In Australia, penguins have to watch out for birds of prey, tiger snakes, lizards, foxes, cats, and rats.

PENGUINS AND PEOPLE

Penguins and people are not always a good mix. Although people enjoy these amazing water birds, penguins reap few benefits from people. For one thing, people and penguins eat some of the same foods. The penguin population requires millions of fish to survive. The more fish people take from the sea, the fewer there are for penguins.

Taking a group of penguins for a walk, this zookeeper is on good terms with his birds.

TOURIST TROUBLE ▼

People who visit penguins in their natural habitat sometimes interrupt the care of eggs and the feeding of chicks, which can be a real hazard in the penguin world.

◀ Royal Penguins

LAMP OIL

At one time penguin fat was used as a source for lamp oil. On the Macquarie Islands of New Zealand, 150,000 Royal Penguins are said to have been killed every year between 1894 and 1914 just to make oil.

FERTILE GROUND

Guano, the droppings of seabirds, is valuable to people and penguins. People use it for fertilizer. Black-footed Penguins in Africa use it for nesting material. Because people have taken so much of the guano, penguins have lost breeding ground.

Oil-soaked penguins await a bath.

These penguins have been cleansed of oil and are now happily heading home.

DEADLY SPILLS

Oil spills are a great danger to penguins. Feathers that are soaked and clogged with oil cannot protect the birds from the cold. If the penguins try to clean off the oil, they can be poisoned. At that point, conservationists often rush to the penguins' rescue and try to save as many as they can.

PROTECTION

Certain penguin species are considered endangered, but now penguins are protected by law. The effort to safeguard them began in the early 1900s. In 1959, twelve nations signed the Antarctic Treaty to save the area and its animals from further destruction.

WHALES & DOLPHINS

LIVING LARGE

It's amazing, but true. Some whales are even larger than the biggest dinosaurs were. Whales have lived on Earth for about 50 million years. As their food supply increased, whales ate more and became bigger over time. The blue whale is the largest animal that has ever lived. It can grow to 100 feet long and weigh about 300,000 pounds. That's as heavy as 25 elephants!

This baby humpback whale, swimming with its mother, might grow as long as 60 feet as an adult and weigh as much as 40 tons. ▶

Spotted dolphins

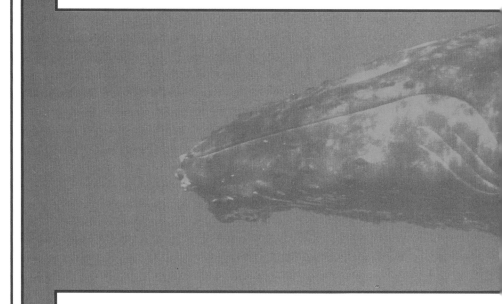

FAST AND FUN ▲

When you think of dolphins, you probably think of fun. You're right! These speedsters are very playful. Ranging from about six feet to 13 feet long, dolphins like to leap clear out of the water and ride the waves made by boats.

Gray whale showing baleen in upper jaw.

TOOTH OR COMB

Cetaceans are grouped according to how they eat. Some have teeth that snag sea creatures. Others, like the big gray whale (left), have comblike structures called baleen. With baleen, whales can filter the sea for food and eat thousands of pounds every day. No wonder they grow to such enormous sizes!

Dolphin with teeth

SOUNDS FISHY

Although they live in water, whales and dolphins are not fish. They are mammals. Like humans, they are warm-blooded. A thick layer of fat, called blubber, helps them keep warm and survive in cold water. Also, cetaceans have lungs rather than gills. They breathe through a blowhole at the top of their head. And, they don't hatch eggs, but give birth to their babies and then nurse them on milk.

◀ This fin whale blows out water from its blowhole.

WATER PIGLETS

The porpoise probably gets its name, which means pig-fish in Latin, from being so short and chubby. Ranging from 3 to 6 feet long, most porpoises aren't as playful or as fast as dolphins. However, Dall's porpoise is known for zipping through the water and kicking up white spray.

Dall's porpoise

TOTALLY TOOTHED

The majority of whales, including all dolphins and porpoises, have teeth. But they don't chew. They swallow their food whole. In fact, most toothed whales only use their teeth to catch and hold their prey.

▲ Dusky dolphins enjoying a meal of anchovies.

◄ Common dolphins are very energetic swimmers, which helps them catch the 10 to 20 pounds of food they eat each day.

THE UNICORN LOOK

It may seem incredible, but the long spear on the head of narwhals is actually a tooth. Narwhals have two teeth, but in the males, the one on the left side grows through the upper lip and reaches up to 10 feet long. Scientists believe that it's used to attract females. Whatever its purpose, this fantastic tusk gives the narwhal the look of a swimming unicorn.

DEEP DIVES ▶

Beluga whales feed by diving deep into the ocean, sometimes over 1,000 feet down. There they munch on fish, squid, crabs, shrimp, clams, and worms.

ZAP AND TRAP ▼

From its large head, the sperm whale produces sound waves that stun the giant 4,000-pound squid living in the ocean depths. The whale then swallows its favorite food whole.

WHALE HUNGRY ▼

Killer whales definitely use their 50 cone-shaped teeth to chew. Also known as *orcas,* a name that comes from Orcus, the Roman god of the underworld, these killers can cut a seal in half. Traveling in packs, they will attack not only fish, but also big baleen whales, dolphins, porpoises, manatees, turtles, and penguins.

FANG FIGHTS

The male sperm whale uses his teeth to fight other males during mating season. The 24 to 30 cone-shaped teeth on each side of the lower jaw grow up to seven inches long and weigh as much as two pounds each.

This sperm whale tooth was scrimshawed, or engraved, in 1877 by whalers.

FILTER FEEDERS

It may seem odd, but there are 10 kinds of whales that don't have any teeth at all. Hanging from their upper jaws are rows of bristled strands called baleen. Made of a material similar to the human fingernail, the baleen acts as a food filter.

Baleen

▲ A humpback whale feeding (note baleen).

SQUEEZE PLAY

Baleen whales eat by taking in a mouthful of water and then "spitting" it out. Anything too large to squeeze through the baleen, such as krill, anchovies, sardines, and herring, is left behind to be swallowed.

KRILL-A-PLENTY

The favorite food of most baleen whales is krill— orange sea creatures that look like shrimp and grow up to two inches long. Scientists estimate there may be six and a half billion tons in the Antarctic Ocean alone! A blue whale eats more than nine tons of krill every day.

SUPER SCOOPERS

Gray whales do not gulp their food. Living close to the shore in the Pacific Ocean, they swim to the bottom of the sea and lie on their side. There they scoop up a mouthful of mud and then force it back out through their baleen. What's left behind is a dinner of crabs and clams.

GULPING GOODIES

Fin whales, as well as blue, Bryde's, humpback, sei, and minke whales, are specially equipped to take huge gulps of krill and fish at one time. On their throats, there are grooves, or pleats, that stretch to allow the throat to expand.

◀ Fin whales feeding on a school of herring.

▼ A humpback's bubble net.

▲
Humpback whales also feed by *lunging* into a school of fish that they've herded into a ball.

BUBBLE TROUBLE

Because humpback whales prefer fish to krill, they sometimes eat in a special way, called bubble-net feeding. The humpback blows air from its blowhole as it swims in a spiral below a school of fish. The bubbles rise in a "net," surrounding the frightened fish. The whale then swims inside the net of bubbles, catching the trapped fish.

THE TALE OF TAILS

Whales and dolphins propel themselves through the water with their tails, which have two strong wings, or *flukes*. Instead of wagging their flukes from side to side like fish, they move them up and down in powerful strokes.

A sperm whale's huge, triangular ▶ flukes are 16 feet across.

The blue whale's 23-foot-long ▶ flukes are relatively small for such an enormous animal.

Humpbacks raise their flukes when diving.
▼

Fin

Tail

Flipper

The humpback whale's flippers are sometimes one-third the length of its entire body.

FABULOUS FLIPPERS

Whales have flippers on each side at the front of their body. In prehistoric days, before whales moved into the water, these flippers were used for walking on land. Whale flippers are now used for steering, braking, and sometimes to knock away an attacker, but not for swimming.

A killer whale's dorsal fin ▲ can grow up to six feet.

The beluga is one of the few ▶ whales without a dorsal fin.

FINTASTIC

Most whales have a stiff fin on their back that helps them stay on course while swimming. Depending on the whale, this dorsal fin can be small or large.

The huge fin whale, which can grow ▶ up to 80 feet, has a tiny dorsal fin.

AIR HEAD

Baleen whales, like the gray whale, have two blowholes.

Looking at a whale, you wouldn't think it had a nose. But it does. Whales have nostrils, called blow-holes. Over millions of years of evolution, whales' nostrils moved to the top of their head, allowing them to breathe by surfacing, rather than by sticking their whole head out of the water.

▲Toothed whales, like this dolphin, have only one blowhole.

The blue whale ▶ shoots a single, thin jet 40 to 50 feet high.

◀ The gray whale blows out a bushy plume 10 to 13 feet high.

BLOW UP

When a whale comes to the surface and exhales, water in the blowhole and moisture in the whale's breath bursts into the air in a marvelous spout. Because whales have different shaped blowholes, they have different shaped spouts.

▲ A right whale sends out two, 16-foot spouts in a V-shape.

ROCK HEAD ▶

Whales do not have completely smooth skin. They are covered with barnacles, worms, lice, and colorful algae. Barnacles grow thickly on gray whales, giving them the appearance of having a rocky surface.

On the right whale, there is a distinctive patch of barnacles, worms, and lice called a "bonnet" or "rock garden." The head accounts for 40% of the whale's entire length.

Blue whale

Sperm whale

BIG HEAD

Some whales have very large heads compared to the rest of their body. Their necks are stiff to keep their large heads steady while they're swimming. For this reason, most whales cannot turn their head from side to side.

A blue whale is one-fourth head and three-fourths body.

The head of a sperm whale is easy to recognize. It is 20-feet long, 10-feet high, and 7-feet wide. Its tooth-filled jaw is 16 feet long.

Right whale

WHALE WATCH

Shown here in relation to one another by size, whales and dolphins vary greatly in shape and color.

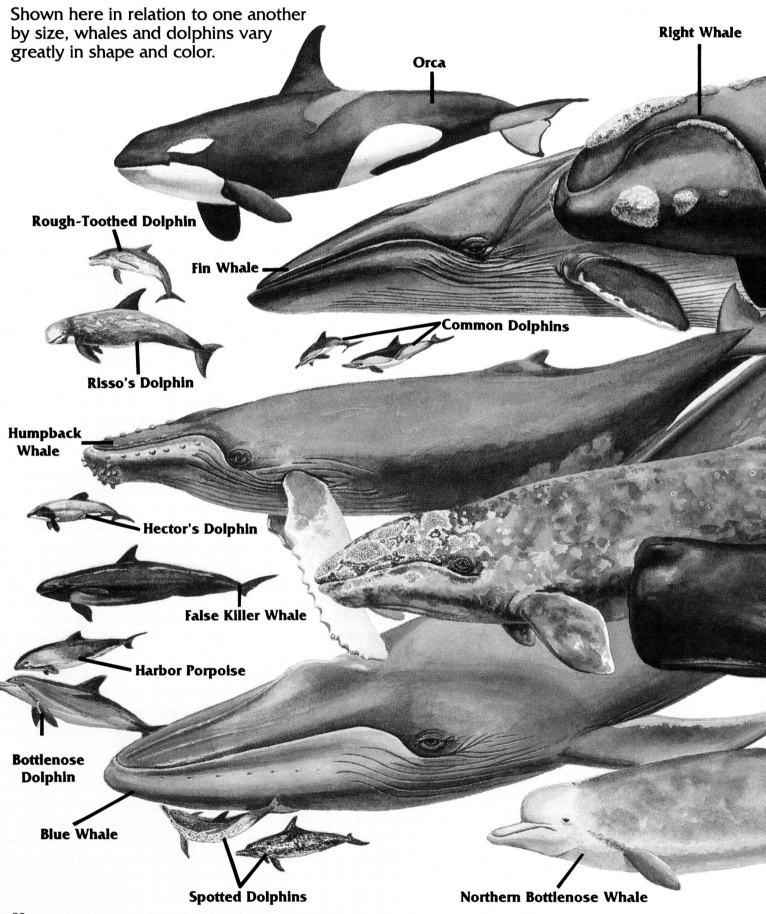

Orca

Right Whale

Rough-Toothed Dolphin

Fin Whale

Risso's Dolphin

Common Dolphins

Humpback Whale

Hector's Dolphin

False Killer Whale

Harbor Porpoise

Bottlenose Dolphin

Blue Whale

Spotted Dolphins

Northern Bottlenose Whale

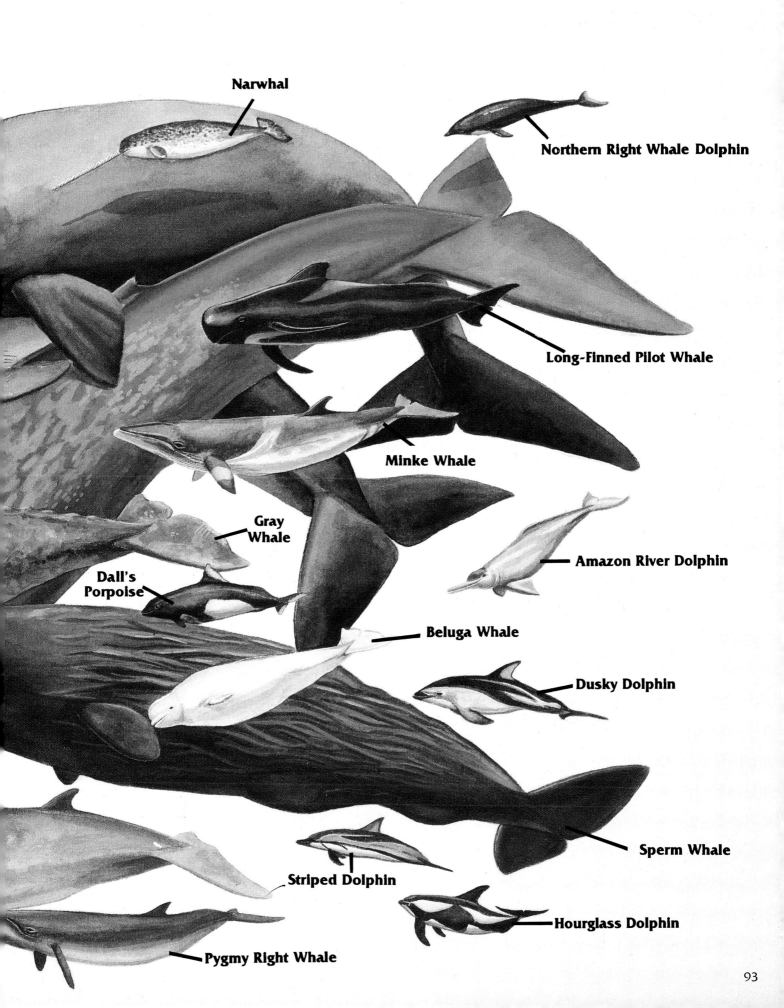

Narwhal

Northern Right Whale Dolphin

Long-Finned Pilot Whale

Minke Whale

Gray Whale

Amazon River Dolphin

Dall's Porpoise

Beluga Whale

Dusky Dolphin

Sperm Whale

Striped Dolphin

Hourglass Dolphin

Pygmy Right Whale

WHAT A BABY!

A baby whale, called a calf, is extremely close to its mother. From the moment of its underwater birth, a calf is totally dependent on her. The two will spend many months together, sometimes years, before the young calf can take care of itself.

The birth of an orca. ▲

▲ A gray whale mother and her calf surface together for air.

SINK OR SWIM

The first thing a newborn whale must do is go to the surface for air, even though it cannot yet swim. Its mother and sometimes another female whale will help it to the surface. Within about a half hour, the baby will be able to swim on its own.

This family of spotted dolphins keeps ▲ their baby under protective cover.

This mother whale and her calf ▼ come up above water for a look around.

COPY CAT CALF

Calves learn by imitating. They turn, dive, and surface right along with their mother. But whale mothers aren't just teachers. They're also playmates. Gray whale mothers play a special game with their babies. They swim underneath them and blow bubbles out their blowhole. This sends little whales into a spin.

BABY LOVE

Because calves are very playful, they sometimes get into trouble. Often aunts will help take care of them, but mothers still watch their babies closely. When a calf disobeys, its mother butts it with her head. She also protects her baby by using her flippers to hold it close to her body.

▲ This baby beluga sticks close to its mother.

FREE RIDE

Calves follow closely at their mother's side. Some keep up by riding their mother's waves and underwater currents. The flow of water over the mother's body helps pull the calf along. For a really easy ride, babies will hang on to their mother's fin.

BABY BLUES

Whale babies grow quickly on their mother's rich milk. Blue whale babies grow the fastest of all. At birth, they can be as long as 23 feet and weigh as much as two tons. They will drink about 44 gallons of milk a day and gain seven pounds an hour. Usually, blue whales grow until they're about 30 years old, and they live to be 60 to 80 years old.

WATER SPORTS

Whales, as big as they are, swim with unusual grace. But swimming is not all they can do. Whales perform aquabatics. They breach, lobtail, sail, surf, and spyhop. Some scientists think that the noise made from lobtailing and breaching may be another way whales communicate. But, maybe it's just whale play.

LOBTAILING ▲

Without warning, a lobtailing whale suddenly points itself straight down into the water. It raises its huge flukes into the air, wags them playfully back and forth a few times, and then slaps them against the water with a sound as loud as a cannon shot. Whales also raise their flukes into the air like sails and glide just beneath the surface on wind power.

Humpback whale

SPYHOPPING

A spyhopping whale sticks its head straight out of the water like a giant periscope and holds it there for 30 seconds or more. It looks around, sometimes turning a full circle, and then disappears. Then it sometimes comes back to do it all over again.

RACING AND CHASING

Dolphins like to swim fast. When a speeding boat passes by, they'll race out in front and ride its bow waves. When racing each other, they'll first leap into the air and then take off after hitting the water. Dolphins also play tag and dance on their tails across the water's surface.

▲ These bottlenose dolphins fly high above the sea.

◀ A spotted dolphin leaps clear of the water and skirts the surface.

▼ SURFING

Right whales swim upstream into strong tidal currents. When they stop swimming, the current sweeps them back to where they started—to do it all over again. Imagine a body-surfer 60-feet long!

BREACHING

To breach, a whale first dives underwater, then throws itself straight up into the air, as high as it can. Some even leap clear of the water. But whales cannot fly, so they fall back into the sea with a loud splash that can be heard for miles.

97

ALL IN THE FAMILY

Most whales are fairly social and like to live in groups. These herds, or *pods*, vary in number and consist of family members and friends. Beluga whales usually live in Arctic waters in large groups that number up to 1,000. However, every few years one or two will follow cold currents as far south as New York City.

◀ A pod of beluga whales.

A pod ▶
of orcas.

ROUND-TRIP TRAVELERS

◀ Many whales migrate constantly, traveling from one region to another to find food, breed, and have their young. Each spring, gray whales leave their winter breeding grounds off the coast of Baja California. They head to the Arctic Ocean, where they feed on krill. In September, they start south again, swimming 24 hours a day to reach their favorite lagoon in time to have their young. The round-trip journey is over 12,000 miles.

BUDDY BAILOUT ▶

Dolphins swim in large herds that sometimes number more than 1,000. They also associate with other whales, such as the right, humpback, and gray whales. Within these groups, dolphins look out after one another. When danger approaches, they send signals. If one member is injured or in distress, they will push it to the surface so it can breathe.

HOME, HOME ON THE SEA

Whales and dolphins live in all the world's oceans and some of its rivers, as well. Some live far out to sea while others hug the shore.

Found in all the world's oceans, from the tropics to the Arctic, orcas usually live in pods numbering 3 to 30, but sometimes they travel in larger herds that number 100.

◀ HERD HUNGER

Group living is safer when enemies like sharks and killer whales are nearby. It also makes it easier for some whales to find and catch food. Species like these humpback whales sometimes gather in large groups and drive fish into a concentrated area. This is called cooperative feeding.

INVISIBLE MAPS

Whales and dolphins navigate by following the hills and valleys on the ocean floor, by tracking the sun, by sensing ocean currents, and by tasting the water from rivers and bays along their journey. They also detect changes in the earth's magnetic field, a sense that acts like an internal compass. This "compass" helps them through even dark, murky water. 99

Gray whale

Right whales have eyes ▶
the size of grapefruits.

SEA SIGHTS AND SOUNDS

Much of the sea is dark all of the time. To get around safely, find food, and to locate one another, whales and dolphins have developed keen senses. Scientists disagree about how well whales can see. Some think they have poor above-water vision and good underwater vision. Others think they see quite well above and below water.

CRY BABIES

Whales have no eyelids. They rely on thick, oily tears to protect their eyes from the effects of seawater and air. Captured dolphins give the impression they are crying. But they aren't. Their tears are flowing to protect their sensitive eyes from drying out.

PINHOLE WONDERS Although they have no ears on the outside of their heads, whales and dolphins have excellent hearing. Tiny pinholes, as narrow as a pencil, are located just behind their eyes. Through these holes, they can pick up sounds from many miles away.

WHALE TALK

The sea is not as silent as it seems. Whales talk to one another by making whistles, clicks, squeaks, squawks, rattles, and groans. People can hear these sounds, too. Male humpback whales sing "songs," which have been taped. People listen to these recordings as they would any other kind of music.

◀ This pilot whale, right behind the mike, tells all.

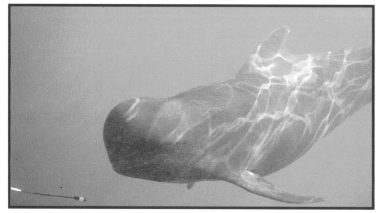

ECHO VISION

Like bats, toothed whales can make sounds to "see" what lies ahead. This sense is called *echolocation*. The whale's sound waves hit an object, such as a school of fish, and the echo bounces back. Echolocation sounds, called *spray*, are so strong that they can stun things, such as fish or other whales. From early on, whales and dolphins learn that they must never "point" their melon toward other whales.

▼ To avoid spraying each other these dolphins swim side by side.

▼ These belugas hang out without pointing their melons at each other.

A REAL WATER MELON

A whale's sounds probably originate in its nasal passages. The large forehead, or melon, found on some whales, like on this bottlenose dolphin, is thought to focus the sounds.

ORCA

LIFETIME COMPANIONS

Orca pods are very much like close families. An orca spends its whole life in the same group and continues to stay attached to its mother. Each pod may also have its own specific way of living, choosing to eat certain things and communicating in ways slightly different from other pods.

FIN TOWERS

How can you tell male and female orcas apart? Male killer whales have really tall—up to six feet— dorsal fins. Females and young orcas have smaller, curved fins that resemble those of dolphins.

▲ TRUE, FALSE KILLERS

Unlike orcas, false killer whales are all black and slender. Sometimes people confuse them with female orcas because their fins are short and hooked.

KILLER CAPERS

Like dolphins, orcas love to play. Although they can weigh as much as 18,000 pounds and grow to 32 feet, they are very athletic. Killer whales can swim 30 miles per hour and can leap and turn quickly. These talents are what makes them so dangerous. They fear nothing and can chase down almost any sea creature.

A spyhopping ▶ killer whale.

This breaching orca shows off its distinctive white patches.

LIFE'S TOO SHORT

Many people believe that orcas should not be held in captivity. In acquariums, orcas tend to live for about 13 years. Compared to those in the wild, who live for 40 to 60 years, their lifetime in captivity is much too short.

This mother and calf ▶ perform a double breach.

IN THE TANK

Orcas, like dolphins, are easily trained. They have large brains and are very intelligent. They are affectionate and gentle, too, and usually cooperate with trainers. Because of their wondrous performances at marine parks, orcas have helped to strengthen the whale protection movement.

KILLING TIME

Some people wonder if the bond formed between trainers and orcas adequately replaces the whales' social life in the wild. They do enjoy having their rubbery skin petted by human hands. But sometimes orcas become so bored that they think up tricks of their own just to kill time.

This killer whale is hanging out with a trainer friend.

NET LOSS

Many dolphins and porpoises get trapped in fishing nets. Unable to surface and breathe air, the water mammals drown. *Drift nets,* some big enough to encircle the city of New York, are set for fish but catch everything. Because the fishermen want only the fish, they simply throw the bodies of the dead dolphins and porpoises back overboard.

WHALES AND PEOPLE

Right whale

Because of their size and speed, whales have few natural enemies besides humans. In the 19th century, people hunted whales to near extinction for oil, baleen, and meat. Baleen was used like plastic is today, in products like brushes and corsets. A few nations still practice whaling, but most have now stopped.

Right whales were first hunted in 12th-century Spain. They are now in danger of extinction.

▼ The vaquita porpoise, like this one, is a common victim of the fisherman's net. There are only a few hundred still living.

TOXIC WATERS

Pollution is the greatest threat whales face today. Oil spills, toxic wastes, and sewage dumping affect the foods that whales eat and become toxins in their systems. Some scientists believe that pollution harms the whale's navigating system, causing some to swim into shallow waters and wash ashore.

These beached pilot ▲ whales are being kept wet by a friendly human.

◀ A researcher rescues a harbor porpoise from a herring net.

In 1988, these volunteers chopped a hole in the Alaskan ice to free two gray whales that were trapped.

An injured humpback whale.

NYLON NICKS

Even nylon fishing lines that float on the sea can severly injure dolphins and whales. The animal gets entangled, and the line cuts through its flesh, sometimes cutting off the dorsal fin.

FRIENDLY FOLKS

Many people and organizations are now working to secure a safer future for dolphins and whales.

MAMMAL GET-TOGETHER

Whale-watching groups go out to sea in hope of meeting whales. Getting close to these magnificent mammals is an exciting experience.

Index

Glossary

Ampullae of Lorenzini: Sensory cells that help sharks detect electrical activity, such as the kind given off by an eel.

Anal Fin: Fin on the rear underside that, along with the dorsal fin, keeps a fish stable in the water.

Blubber: Thick layer of fat that protects whales and other marine mammals from the cold.

Brooding: Period when parents of penguins or other birds protect chicks and keep them warm.

Brood Patch: Featherless area on a penguin's belly.

Camouflage: Way that an animal disguises and protects itself by appearing to blend into its surroundings.

Carnivore: Animal that eats the flesh of other animals.

Cartilage: Soft, flexible gristle that joins one bone to another; human ears and noses are made up of cartilage.

Caudal Fin: Fin that helps a shark or other fish move forward; also known as tail fin.

Cetacea: Group of warm-blooded sea mammals that includes whales, dolphins, and porpoises.

Cold-blooded: Having a body temperature that is not regulated internally but adapts to the temperature of surrounding air or water; reptiles and amphibians are cold-blooded.

Copepods: Type of plankton that are barely visible, lobster-like creatures.

Crop: Special pouch in a penguin's throat used to store undigested food; a chick fits its bill inside its parent's mouth to retrieve the food.

Crustacean: Class of joint-legged animals with a hard outer covering; includes lobsters and crabs.

Denticles: Hard, teeth-like scales on a shark.

Dorsal Fin: Large fin on the upper back of a fish that keeps the fish from rolling over.

Elasmobranch: Family that sharks belong to.

Evolve: To gradually change or develop.

Eyespot: False eye, larger than a real eye, located on a fish near the tail and used to fool predators into thinking that the fish is too big to eat.

Fledging: The growth stage of penguin chicks (or other chicks) when they grow adult feathers and are ready to leave their parents and go to sea.

Food Chain: Series of living things in which each feeds upon the one below it and in turn is eaten by the one above it; cycle repeats itself until the tiniest animal eats the bacteria that is left behind from the largest animal.

Fry: Baby, or young, fish.

Gills: Breathing organs of fish and other water animals; most fish have one pair of gill slits, but sharks have five to seven pairs.

Herbivore: Animal that eats only fruits, plants, and vegetables.

Hibernate: To rest, or sleep, and remain inactive through the winter; animals that hibernate survive on the food stored in their bodies until spring.

Incubate: To keep eggs warm, by sitting on them, in order to hatch them.

Lateral Line: Line of canals from a fish's head to tail that sends messages to the brain, warning it that other objects or creatures are nearby; canals receive messages from vibrations in the water.

Migrate: To travel or move.

Mollusk: Animal that has a soft, muscular body but no backbone; snails, mussels, and clams are mollusks.

Molt: To shed skin, feathers, hair, or hard outside covering; penguins replace feathers by molting.

Nictitating Membrane: Lower lid that covers and helps protect a shark's eye in dangerous situations.

Nursery: Place where a mother fish, penguin, or other animal, lays her eggs.

Pectoral Fins: Fins on both sides of a fish's chest that are used for balance.

Pelvic Fin: Center fin on a fish's underside that helps it to balance, steer, and stop.

Plankton: Tiny animals and plants living in the sea that are the basic food for larger sea animals.

Predator: Animal that hunts other animals for food.

Prey: An animal that is hunted by other animals for food.

Pup: Baby shark.

Rookery: Large, noisy gathering where penguins look for mates and breed.

Roost: To rest, or perch; also, the place where an animal sleeps, hibernates, and has babies.

Serrated: Notched edge, like on saws or steak knives; a shark's teeth are serrated.

Spawn: To produce eggs; a female fish places her eggs in the water, and the male fertilizes them.

Toboggan: Method by which penguins move fast and glide, by lying belly-down and pushing with their feet and flippers.

Ultrasound: High-pitched noises that humans cannot hear.

Venom: Poisonous liquid secreted by some animals.

Warm-blooded: Having a high body temperature that is regulated internally and is not affected by surroundings; birds and mammals are warm-blooded.